T0064501

I'M TOO OLD FOR THIS SH*T!

Quit Office Politics and Be the CEO of YOU!

VICTORIA WRIGHT

BALBOA.PRESS
A DIVISION OF HAY HOUSE

Balboa Press books may be ordered through booksellers or by contacting:

Balboa Press
A Division of Hay House
1663 Liberty Drive
Bloomington, IN 47403
www.balboapress.com.au
AU TFN: 1 800 844 925 (Toll Free inside Australia)
AU Local: 0283 107 086 (+61 2 8310 7086 from outside Australia)

Print information available on the last page.

ISBN: 978-1-5043-2452-6 (sc)
ISBN: 978-1-5043-2456-4 (e)

Balboa Press rev. date: 02/17/2021

CONTENTS

Dedicated to

Bill, Chloé, Max, Lulu, and Beau

Mum and Dad

You are each and collectively my inspiration.

To my darling husband, soulmate, and best friend, Bill. We have weathered the trials and turbulence of this thing called life together for over three decades now. While it hasn't always been smooth sailing, inevitably we have always caught each other at the right time and are now stronger than ever, navigating the choppy waters with clarity, determination, and unflappable spirit.

To my darling baby girl, Chloé. The first second I held you, I experienced love like never before. I would do anything for you, my angel. You are incredibly intelligent, caring, and beautiful inside and out. Be strong, sweetheart. Don't let anyone or anything stop you from being the beautiful, amazing woman you are. The world is your oyster.

To my amazing boy, Max. You have always been my little man, so smart and full of character. I love you, too, angel. Stay focused on your goals. You confirm my belief in the power of thought and mental toughness because despite your tender years, I have witnessed you manifest so much already. Achieving your dreams is a given.

To Lulu and Beau, my gorgeous fur babies. Your incredible love and loyalty, together with the joy you bring to all of us, inspires my journey, so I can help other beautiful animals less fortunate than the two of you.

To Mum and Dad, my first teachers. My story is just that, *my* story and you have been a big part of it – shaping me through the good times and not so good times. Thank you for the love and support you have always given me.

I have written this book to create positive change, uplift, and inspire people to challenge their current paradigms. To consider that there is life outside a standard corporate job (Just Over Broke) and that there is ultimate freedom to be gained by clearing the years of nonsense conditioned into our psyches.

ABOUT THE AUTHOR

Victoria Wright is a consultant, business owner, investor and network marketer.

Over the years, she took the usual path of going to school and getting a good job to provide for her family. But she just knew there was more to life.

This is her story of how to leave the corporate rat-race behind for good. Through her story, she shares valuable insight into how our internal belief systems may be holding us back from achieving the life we dream of. Victoria explains how she and millions of others have said goodbye to the corporate grind to achieve financial and team freedom through a vehicle that is available to all. However to be successful, one must have an open mind and be willing to discard old limiting beliefs.

An easy, enjoyable read, this book gives you honest insight and inspiration. It guides you on a journey of your own reflection, questioning, and action to achieve the life you really want.

Victoria lives in Sydney, Australia.

PRELUDE

"Hi. Just fill out this form, buzz me when you've finished, then take a seat, and wait for me to come back," said the no more than twenty-three-year-old recruitment consultant. Startled by her rudeness, I steadily took a seat, pen poised between my thumb and forefinger above the form ... and froze.

What the hell am I doing here? I wondered. I'm in my forties, and my job as a executive in a major company was made redundant several months ago. I've lost count of the number of applications, emails, phone calls, LinkedIn messages, and interviews I have had since then.

"Get a degree. You'll get a better job and earn great money," they said.

I have two degrees, led teams and managed businesses with turnover in the hundreds of millions, raised two children who are now young adults, maintained a marriage through financial and emotional highs and lows, and cared for my elderly parents. And now my financial future, and to an extent my identity, is resting in the hands of someone less than half my age!

Placing the clipboard and pen on the counter, I collected my bag and headed for the exit.

"I'm too old for this sh*t!"

ACKNOWLEDGEMENTS

To my dear friend Rachel, your support, amazing ideas, and no BS approach gave me the reboot I needed! I'm so glad to be sharing this ride with you.

To my darling Athelfi, thank you for your unconditional love, laughter, and support. And for igniting that spark all those years ago that is now burning like wildfire!

To my trainer and mentor, Gordon, thank you for sharing your deep knowledge and experience in applied psychology in a way that has inspired a lifelong passion of reflection and personal challenge.

To my coach, Jim, it is so nice to connect with someone who just gets it! Thank you for your patience through the various iterations of me.

To all the authors of personal development, financial education, and network marketing books who have long inspired me.

To the school of life and hard knocks, thank you for making me tough, resilient, and able to conquer the twists and turns encountered on my journey so far.

WHO AM I?

I am a forty-something wife, mum, and former corporate employee from Sydney Australia. My life was fairly normal by most Western standards. I am an only child and had a normal, albeit uneventful childhood followed by the typical foray into adulthood—study, corporate career, marriage, mortgage and children. Life carried on with its inevitable ups and downs, but overall, I felt I was doing what I was supposed to be doing. But something just wasn't right. I began to see the ugly side of corporate life. Our income, whilst good, did not seem to allow us to get ahead. As income increased, so did outgoings. I felt I was on a treadmill and getting nowhere fast. Apart from not achieving my goals financially, my health, both physically and mentally, was also not where I wanted it to be.

I knew there had to be a better way. I decided to find that way and realised that the biggest hurdle to achieving the life I wanted was the thing between my ears! In other words, my mind was filled with limiting beliefs developed through the experiences of my life, and they needed to be challenged and let go. Through a series of experiences, some by choice and others not, I learnt how to remove limiting beliefs and replace them with those which serve me. This is not to say I see the world through rose-coloured glasses and dismiss reality. Far from it! My training in hypnotherapy and Neuro-Linguistic Programming (NLP) helped me to shift years of deep-seated self-doubt and feelings of inadequacy that held me back. It also opened my eyes to the potential for financial and time freedom through network marketing, something I had wanted but previously failed at due to subconscious beliefs that although I liked the concept, believed it would never work for me.

My life now is very different from the so-called normal that is expected by society. I escaped the corporate treadmill and am happily my own boss with multiple income streams—consulting, investments, online training and network marketing. Most important, I am happy! Happy with the freedom of being 100 per cent responsible for myself, no bosses or staff to deal with. Happy with the variety I have in my days. And I am happy that I can work from wherever I want and have income that allows me to enjoy my life and spend time doing what I love.

More details of my story follow within this book where relevant to provide context.

My only wish is that I'd arrived here sooner!

WHY THIS BOOK?

I wrote this book for everyone frustrated with their "lot in life"—whether from a work, financial, or lifestyle perspective—and feel trapped by circumstances. Notably, frustrated by the need to earn an income to pay the bills yet not having the time and often the energy to enjoy the fruits of their labour.

I believe many of you will resonate with much of what the following pages discuss:

> Women—generally over forty—who find themselves to have hit the proverbial "glass ceiling" prescribed by the powerbrokers within a corporation, suddenly faced with an uncertain future predicated by corporate restructures, inequalities, and politics.

> Men—generally aged from forty-five—who find themselves in a similar situation with the added emotional burden of feeling they have somehow "failed" themselves and their families by not achieving the level of corporate and financial success they thought

would just happen by following the usual trajectory of getting a good job and climbing the corporate ladder.

People who have invested their life's savings into a business, such as a retail franchise, only to find themselves working around the clock to break even as they deal with a fickle casual workforce, slowed foot traffic in shopping centres, and ever-changing consumer preferences.

People employed in manual or physically demanding work, such as construction or nursing, and find their abilities to keep up the pace with increasing years tough and are facing an uncertain retirement as savings plans may not have eventuated as planned.

Women who put their careers on hold to raise a family and experience a major upheaval, such as divorce, and find themselves having to get a job for the first time in decades. Many find they lack the skills required today, and the jobs they can perform can be filled by much younger talent at a significantly lower rate of pay.

People who have tried network marketing and failed— also known as quitting. People who diligently made lists of hundreds of their "closest friends," attended every event, and were active on social media only to quit several months later because it just wasn't working for them.

And those who have never considered another way, another lifestyle than the corporate nine-to-five treadmill and how to be truly financially free.

The book is divided into five parts. Part 1 deals with the old paradigm of going to school, getting a job, working hard for forty years, and then retiring. Part 2 discusses how those of us who feel too old for this sh*t got to where we are. Part 3 shows how network marketing may be a way to achieve financial and time freedom. Part 4 deals with the mindset shifts required to achieve freedom, starting with freedom from the limiting beliefs inside our minds. And part 5 provides practical steps to help you overcome limiting beliefs, all of which are based on my learning and experiences.

This book is a fairly easy read as it is just my story. There is no right or wrong. This book is simply my opinion based on my experience.

My hope is for those of you who can see yourselves—or at least part of yourselves—through my story, you will identify any beliefs or attitudes that may be preventing you from being truly happy by living the life you really want, and work toward positive change.

PART 1
THE OLD PARADIGM

We trained hard—but it seemed that every time we were beginning to form up into teams we were reorganised. I was to learn later in life that we tend to meet any new situation by reorganising, and what a wonderful method it can be for creating the illusion of progress while actually producing confusion, inefficiency, and demoralisation.

—Petronius Arbiter

THE WORLD OF WORK HAS CHANGED

As far back as five hundred years before Christ, the Greek philosopher Heraclitus argued that "life is flux" and that the only constant in life is change.

The world of work has changed significantly during the past few decades—some changes for good, and others not so good, depending on your situation. Positive changes include increasing diversity of employees in the workforce; more flexibility for employees, including work-from-home and job-share arrangements; and a higher focus by organisations on having a meaningful purpose for their employees to believe in.

Conversely, the rapid pace of change characterised by globalisation, continued technological and digital advances, offshoring, and industrial shifts have also resulted in serious disruptions to the way employees work. The gig economy appears here to stay, with an increased prevalence of short-term, contract, and temporary work arrangements. This is great for freelancers and those comfortable with not knowing where they will be working next and when they will receive income. But for people who are used to a steady, permanent job at a standard location with familiar faces and a regular pay cheque, the gig economy requires a considerable shift in mindset and lifestyle.

Everyone will agree the COVID-19 pandemic of 2020 impacted not only the way we work but the fabric of work entirely. The unprecedented events surrounding the pandemic left millions of employees without a job and forced them to rely on government payments for the first time in their lives. Businesses downsized or closed, causing widespread financial and mental stress for thousands and thousands of people who never considered their safety net could be pulled out from under them without warning.

Acknowledging that the only constant is change may help us deal with the reasons our work lives are vastly different today than they were decades ago. But it does not make the issues facing today's workforce any easier to navigate.

TALKIN' ABOUT MY GENERATION

Most of us are common with the terms "Generation Xers," "millennials," and "baby boomers," but what do they mean? These terms refer to groups of people born around the same time and exhibit similar characteristics and values largely dependent on the environment and influences at the time.

Generations are shown to display similar characteristics particularly with regard to values, attitudes, and expectations around work and finances. This is largely because they experienced similar environmental impacts, such as war, political influences, and communication channels. Obviously each individual is different. However, there are definite trends common among cohorts born and living through various periods in history.

Following is a snapshot of generations and the most common characteristics exhibited by each.

	Traditionalists/ Maturists	Baby Boomers	Generation X	Generation Y/ Millennials	Generation Z
Years born	1922–1945	1946–1965	1966–1980	1981–1994	1995–2015
Characteristics	Loyal; respectful of authority; hierarchical; risk-averse; hard-working; financially conservative; frugal; values security, privacy, and familiar environments/ activities	Optimistic, idealistic, educated, loyal, opinionated, lives to work, bases self-worth on work ethic, loyal to employer, competitive, goal-centric, focused, disciplined	Works to live, sceptical, resourceful, independent, pragmatic, adaptable, craves independence, eager to learn, thrives on flexibility, entrepreneurial, sees education as necessary to succeed	Technologically savvy, empowered, confident, collaborative, fully transparent, shares everything, desires to make an impact, values diversity, loves technology, does not perform best in a traditional work environment	Sophisticated media and computer users, more internet savvy, ambitious, multitasks

WHAT THE FUTURE HOLDS FOR GENERATION X

As a member of Generation X, born in the 1970s, my perspectives on life were shaped not only by my parents but by other influences around me at the time.

It is no surprise that advances in medicine and a focus on health and wellness have led to people living longer and generally healthier lives. The retirement system, however, is still based on previous generations who didn't live as long, so the combination of an aged pension and superannuation/401(k) savings are generally no longer enough for today's generation.

Things are much different today. As people live longer, the current financial model for retirement is unlikely to be sufficient for a large number of people to live a comfortable lifestyle when they finish their careers. The traditionalist generation and baby boomers were accustomed to cradle-to-grave benefits either from the companies they worked for or from the government. This included medical care and retirement savings. In today's economy, job security is more the exception than the rule, and Generation Xers are the ones hurting the most financially. Why is it so tough for those of us born between 1966 and 1980? We aren't quite at retirement age, yet we don't have the freedom and enthusiasm of younger workers fresh out of school, who have fewer obligations and more flexibility. We are overloaded with responsibility—raising families; trying to save for the future; looking after our parents, who are living longer … and it all takes money!

When I started in the workforce, jobs were relatively plentiful. We did the usual thing of working our way up but then were hit with shocks like the burst of the tech bubble and the global financial crisis. This left many of us feeling shaken and concerned about the future. We may not necessarily like the jobs we have or the income we earn, but we lack the confidence, opportunity, or flexibility to change. According to Mercer's report *Inside Employees' Minds* (2011), more and more people are disengaged at work. In essence, we are stuck. Yet companies persist in talking proudly about their own achievements through the results of employee engagement surveys, underpinned by questions that inevitably lead employees to giving the answers executives want to hear in fear of retribution.

AGEISM IN THE WORKFORCE

As a Gen Xer, I have experienced and witnessed ageism in the workforce first hand. According to Diversity Council Australia, people can start to be affected by age discrimination in the workplace at forty-five years of age. Stereotypes still exist around older people being slow, less digitally capable, and unlikely to remain with a company due to looming retirement. For these reasons, not only do older people find it harder to secure a job, they are often encouraged to take redundancy packages or even tapped on the shoulder to move on.

The largest group of people on government unemployment benefits in Australia are aged fifty-five or older. This group has been described to be wasting savings, accessing superannuation to pay off their mortgages, and becoming part of the "pension poor" cohort. It is a fact that it takes an older person longer to find new employment after losing a job than a younger person, and this can have significant impact on finances, health, and mental well-being.

There are countless stories of people with successful careers losing their jobs and becoming virtually unemployable because of their age. Whilst it is positive that governments and lobby groups are working to develop and maintain policies to reduce ageism in the workforce, the fact remains that a significantly large number of people will not have sufficient savings or superannuation to have a comfortable retirement when securing stable income later in life is difficult for many.

And if 2020 has taught us anything, it is that virtually no one is immune to unemployment when a global shock, such as the COVID-19 pandemic, hits. Industries from airlines and hospitality to retail and even professional services were forced to stand down staff for indefinite periods, make thousands of jobs redundant, and close operations altogether. The flow on effect is huge. Financial markets took a huge hit, and this had direct impact on the retirement savings of millions.

FINDING A JOB IN YOUR FORTIES, FIFTIES, AND BEYOND

For those forty- and fifty-somethings fortunate enough to have survived the latest corporate restructure, it is worthwhile to consider a what-if scenario should the situation arise that they have to seek alternative employment. Globalisation and the gig economy have removed a lot of roles from organisations. Transactional roles are offshored or outsourced as companies realise the economic benefits that can be achieved by utilising workers in emerging countries, paying a fraction of what it costs to employ skilled locals.

That won't happen to you, right? Surely by the time you've reached your forties, the whole getting a job thing is a walk in the park for you. Unfortunately, no. Research continues to show that older workers face unemployment for longer periods of time than younger workers.

Like work itself, the process of finding a job has changed. No longer are we scouring the classified advertisements in the weekend newspaper for our next career moves. These days everything is online—and I mean *everything!*

Job advertisements are found online across various websites, such as Seek, Monster and Indeed. And on top of that, you need to "get social." According to *Fortune* magazine, at least 500 million people use LinkedIn, and there are over ten million active job listings on the platform at any one time.

And when I say social, I *mean* social. Recruiters and employers will scour the internet to check you out before they decide whether to call you. And it can be a case of "damned if you do, damned if you don't." Employers may screen you according to your social media profile. You might be too boring or too outlandish; you may face indirect discrimination if you show photos of children; you may be judged based on your looks, age, or gender. The list goes on and on. Conversely, if you do not have a social media presence, there is a significant chance you will be overlooked entirely. An entire industry has been built around creating the ideal LinkedIn profile. Millions of dollars are being handed over to help you get a job.

Well, if I'm not nailing it on social media, my résumé will be able to explain who I am and how I will be a great asset to the company, right? Again the answer is a categorical no. For a start, recruiters and employers may not even read your résumé before sending the, "Thanks but no thanks" email. Algorithms, not humans, are scanning your résumé for keyword matches. You can attempt to tailor your résumé to include the necessary keywords to match the job advertisement, but the time involved in doing this, and the sheer volume of applications passing through the system, make the chances of receiving an acknowledgement of your application, let alone a response from a human, extremely slim. It is rare to receive a call about a job application, so what hope do you have of selling yourself to a prospective employer if you can't even talk to one? Worse, do you really want to be working for those who cannot make a decision?

If, however, you somehow managed to outsmart the algorithm and secure an interview, congratulations! You're in the minority. So what's next?

As described in the Prelude, the experience of meeting with recruiters, who are generally much younger than us, can be confronting if not downright humiliating. But get over it. This is today's reality! Recruitment consultants, like any sales representative, are hungry for commissions, and if you are not the best "product" to present to their clients, forget it. In other words, you have become a commodity, or "pawn," in their game.

We know we are more than qualified and capable of performing the job. Yet our palms still sweat at the thought of having to prove our worth, skills and abilities to a complete stranger. What if you are more than capable of performing a job but cannot check every box on the position description, or you do not perform well in interviews?

The thought crosses your mind, *Are they serious about me, or am I simply a "filler" to make the preferred candidate stand out?* How many of you have experienced this … made it through rounds of applications, psychometric tests, and interviews only to make it to the final interview and receive a response the next day, "Thank you so much. However, the other candidate had more relevant experience." Yeah, right! Then you begin to question whether in fact the job advertised actually existed.

The fact that the recruiter will more than likely be significantly younger than you is only the beginning. The reality is for Generation X, our next boss is likely to be the same age as one of our children. Think seriously about this for a minute. How does this make you feel? Can you really cope with this? Think of the all the life and work experiences you've had, the battles you've won, could you possibly report to someone who is wearing Gucci but likely still living at home and has not had to deal with the ups and downs of family drama, financial loss, and hard work that you have?

Without flattering ourselves, many Gen Xers and baby boomers could run rings around the current cohort of millennials. However, the fact remains that older workers are working for the younger generation—if they are lucky!

You know you are more than capable, but the reality is you are likely overqualified. All the hard-fought experience is now working against you. Companies want employees to advance their objectives, yet interviewers want to hire people who won't threaten their careers. So what happens? Younger, less-experienced candidates are hired. Like it or not, prospective employers may see your qualifications and experience as a personal threat to their advancement within the company.

Then if you do happen to make it to the pointy end, how do you manage salary negotiations in today's world? Regardless of gender, studies show that by your forties, you're likely to have reached as much money as you will make in your corporate career. Men's salaries peak around the age of forty-eight, and women's close off around the age of thirty-nine. This is largely due to job choice and family responsibilities as salaries expand equally across the genders until the age of thirty, when many women tend to have children and temporarily leave the workforce.

And when you're already fighting to get a job at your age, the bargaining power to negotiate salary is reduced. Push too hard and you may find yourself out of the game.

PERFORMANCE REVIEWS: REPORT CARDS FOR ADULTS

You're hired! Okay, so you've proven me wrong. You've successfully meandered the process of beating algorithms, passing psych assessments, several rounds of interviews with recruiters and employers, and you have secured your new role. Well done!

On your first day you are walked around the floor, being introduced to various departments by someone you think went to school with your daughter. Then a few months in, it's time for your quarterly performance review. Really? Are we still going there?

When I see performance reviews, my mind immediately reverts to my son's primary school report.

> Attendance: Meets expectations

> Homework: Below expectations

> General comments: Max needs to focus more.

These relics of the industrial age are dead in today's workplace, yet they persist as a means of controlling employees and their salaries. Seriously, if a manager and employee cannot have regular, open dialogue without the need to scale, benchmark, and document on an arbitrary chart, there is clearly something wrong. Perhaps it is the human resources managers who insist on this antiquated process for knowledge workers to display their relevance and utilise skills taught at university.

The fact that employee pay increases and bonuses are often determined by the results of performance reviews can contribute to the ugly beast of office politics as people will fight to ensure they receive "higher marks" than a colleague, the prize being a premium place on the performance matrix, translating to salary increases and promotion. In many cases, there are instructions from human resources informing line managers to be extremely frugal with high scores. The reason for this is high scores are supposed to lead to increased responsibilities, promotions, and incomes for employees. However, the reality is, no matter how hard you work, how impressive your results may be, the corporate system makes it very difficult to gain the recognition and salary you deserve.

Give me a break! Why can't we just have an adult conversation anymore?

IS YOUR TONGUE SORE?

How many of us have bite marks on our tongues from all the things you wanted to say at work but didn't?

With the whole performance review process, corporations tell us it is all about improving our development, and we need to be open to feedback and feel comfortable providing feedback to others.

Easier said than done!

Have you ever given real, honest, often unpalatable feedback to a superior and lived to tell the tale? If you have, you are among a select few brave enough to put their positions and incomes on the line to speak their minds.

Instead, we have developed a collective culture of staying silent and just putting up with office politics, pointless meetings, being micromanaged, overanalysed, and justifying our every move.

Please do not get the wrong impression of me. I'm an extremely positive, grateful, and generous person. Whilst these sections may appear somewhat negative, I am simply demonstrating that many people experience these situations and feelings and that you are not alone.

REDUNDANCY

For some, the thought of a redundancy or severance payout is the answer to all their problems. The issue is, though, is once the government takes its share in tax, there's about half left. Then after you use your payout to pay off loans and debts (usually not the mortgage), you realise that there isn't much left over, and you still need to eat.

You have a few months off. Maybe you go on a short getaway, spend your days doing classes at the gym and meeting for coffee with friends who don't work a traditional job. And then you begin to wonder why your massive payout is not covering your ongoing costs of living.

Despite the financial benefit, redundancy can have serious social and emotional impacts. The psychological downturn following a redundancy can be crippling. After the initial excitement of supposed freedom, cash, and new horizons fades, you may start to feel dejected, worthless, and dare I say, redundant. These feelings are exacerbated if it is not a legitimate redundancy but rather a "gentle" way for a company to signal that you are no longer required.

Feelings of shame and embarrassment can soon overtake feelings of elation. Reflection on the way the whole experience transpired can often reveal politics we deliberately avoided simply to maintain the status quo and our jobs.

For many people, however, their identities are inextricably linked to their careers. To be told that their positions have been made redundant is akin to the death of part of their identities. Being ushered into an office and seeing an envelope passed across the desk is devastating to many people. After years of exceeding key performance indicators, building strong teams and sacrificing hours of family time for work, it has all come down to this—an envelope.

Genuine or not, redundancy definitely causes those affected to experience a high degree of uncertainty about their futures. Uncertainties about their financial situations are generally the first consideration. "Will I find another job?" "Will I lose my home?" "Will my partner leave me?"

The initial shock can have a significant effect on an individual. The situation may seem surreal. You may walk out of the office with your cardboard box (á la *Jerry Maguire*!) and then be elated as you open that envelope while sitting in your car. "Wow, now I can take my family on that dream holiday. I can upgrade the back deck. I can send my son to university. I can …" But as you pull into the driveway, a dull ache starts in the pit of your stomach as you approach the front door, knowing you have to admit to your family and yourself that you are, "No longer required."

People experience feelings of denial and anger, which are completely normal under the circumstances. However, as mentioned previously, a more serious effect of redundancy is depression, especially if your job was a significant part of your identity and social network. Financial pressures may exacerbate this, particularly if you are finding it difficult to secure new employment.

WHO AM I, AND WHY AM I TELLING YOU THIS?

So here may be a little late to introduce myself, but I believe it was important it to set the scene.

I was born in the early 1970s in a middle-class suburb of Sydney, Australia. I am the only child of parents who came from a very small country town in central-west New South Wales.

My parents are part of the "silent generation," or "traditionalists." In other words, children of the Great Depression. They each saw first-hand the hardship and struggle their parents had in providing for their very large families. Then as they grew into adults, their upbringing taught them that unlike the previous generation, who had fought to change the system, my parents were of the generation focused on working within the system.

This was demonstrated by their strong work ethic and by keeping their heads down and working hard, hence earning the label "silent generation." By nature, they were frugal. It was not uncommon to hear them remark, "So and so is extravagant," simply because a neighbour had discarded an electrical appliance that was no longer operational. In contrast, my parents chose to maximise the value of everything. I describe their behaviour as hoarding. But then again, who doesn't need at least three broken toasters, a couple of kettles with frayed cords, and four lawnmowers? None operational, but way too good to throw away!

My parents were a little older, having me relatively late for their generation and, as mentioned, grew up in a very small country town. My father moved to Sydney when his parents divorced. This led my mother to leave her hometown and join him and my grandmother in Sydney. I am eternally grateful that I was born in Sydney for the opportunities a large city provided me.

As a child I always followed the rules. Being an only child, I was extremely quiet, well-behaved, and dare I say, boring! I contribute this to their extremely protective—borderline suffocating—parenting style. I was seen but definitely not heard!

I didn't say much growing up, but boy did I listen. And a lot of what I heard focused on money and an apparent disdain for anyone who had more of it than us. Comments frequently made in my home included:

> "Big-timers."

> "They have too much money."

> "Silvertails."

"There's no way for the average man to get ahead."

"Just get a job, and have a small, steady amount coming in week after week."

And so I listened … and obeyed.

As an only child and loner (I'm not seeking sympathy here, just stating the facts), I didn't have many friends at school and took solace in books. I loved to read and loved to learn. In fact, reading random sections of the *Encyclopaedia Britannica* was my favourite thing in the whole world.

Perhaps this led me to achieving excellent results at school. Despite going to the local high school, where I was the, "fat, smart kid," and bullied incessantly, for some reason I was able to channel my focus and achieved dux of each year during my six years of high school.

"Go to university and become a lawyer," my teachers said.

"All of these knowledge boxes who go to university can't get a job," my parents said.

"Why don't you become a hairdresser? That's a nice trade for a girl," my father suggested.

Thinking back now, I cannot understand this logic, and I use that term loosely. You have a daughter who clearly has intelligence, yet you know deep down you don't want her to earn more than you. So consciously or subconsciously, you keep her down.

I ended up doing very well in my final year of high school and received an offer to study at university. However, my confidence and self-esteem were so low that I could not imagine sitting in those huge lecture halls, being a small fish in a big pond. Looking back, it was probably more the constant negativity around education, money, and success imparted on me by my parents that dissuaded me from going to university. It was my fear of failure that stopped me from even considering doing and being something different.

I did not want to be a hairdresser! The thought of touching someone else's hair and having to make small talk terrified me. So I did the next best thing. I was awarded a scholarship to a private business college and trained to become a secretary. So traditional!

As history dictated, I was dux of business college, blitzing my words per minute on the manual typewriter and in shorthand. I landed a job as a junior secretary with a firm of chartered accountants the day after graduation. With this, my first step on the "treadmill" of minimal pay, unpaid overtime, long days, politics, harassment, rules for some and not for others, told when I could take time off, was taken. And just like my parents and millions of others, I began the tried and tested tradition of trading time for money. Although more times than not, I traded more time than the money I received.

Years went by, and I decided to move from job to job to better myself. I worked in the private and public sectors. I was forced to join whatever superannuation fund the company I worked for at the time was aligned with. And I was content.

I bought a property, married the love of my life, had two beautiful children, and even purchased an off-the-plan investment property on the advice of a financial planner, And then something happened.

As the *Wall Street Journal* reported the demise of Lehman Brothers and Merrill Lynch, the shockwaves started to reverberate across the world. Overnight, our home, which we thought was an asset, was valued significantly less than we had paid for it. Our off-the-plan investment property, which we were advised to "Sell before settlement and make tens of millions of dollars," was, in fact, worth hundreds of thousands of dollars less than what we purchased it for. We couldn't lease it to a tenant at a rate high enough to over the repayments, and we were struggling to sell it.

I had two very young children and was working casually at the time. Even with my husband's salary, we just couldn't keep pace with the bills—two mortgages, car, utilities, phones, insurance, food, childcare …

What was happening?

We were broke! Flat-out broke!

We needed more money, and we needed it fast! The constant calls from creditors demanding payment for overdue bills were taking their toll on us and was impacting our health and relationship. So I decided to do the "logical" thing and get a full-time job. Remember, the only experience I had at this stage was in secretarial work. I took a temporary position that turned into a permanent one.

So despite the "minute" facts that I had to get up at the crack of dawn, pull my two babies out of bed, drag them to before-school care, drive halfway across the city to my "dream job" and work as an executive assistant to the CFO of a publicly listed company, I seriously thought I'd hit the jackpot. I had a steady, regular income. My income just about covered all the bills we had. Life was sweet!

I worked extremely long hours, hardly saw my two beautiful children, and often relied on my parents to help out when the before- and after-school fees got a little too high. Yes, I was "living the dream." Indeed, living the dream even when I had to work the Saturday of my young son's birthday, which coincidentally is also my husband's birthday. But that was okay because my job was keeping our heads above water. Right?

This pattern went on for a few years. As I watched those around me moving through the corporate ranks, I thought, *That should have been me. Had my parents not been so negative about university and I had more self-esteem, I would have a degree and been a highly paid executive.*

Oh well, I thought, *better late than never!*

So while working full time and being a wife and mother to two young children, I completed my first degree.

And my plan worked! I graduated, applied for a promotion at my company, and got it. I now officially had the title "manager" and was on top of the world!

Not a lot changed, however. I didn't have any staff to manage. I still worked extremely long hours. I still spent a lot of time away from my children, and my salary didn't increase by much.

But finally, I was on the "ladder."

By this time, I'd moved companies. I became a "national manager," had a team to manage, and earned a higher income. Again I thought, *This is working*.

I was absolutely kicking goals at my new company. Implementing new processes led to huge efficiencies and cost savings, receiving resounding applause from our clients and partners, expanding my team, and winning company awards! I'd made it!

And so I thought, *I did one degree and moved up the ladder. Surely if I do another one, I'll get to the top!* I mean, I was doing what I was supposed to do, wasn't I? I had not one but two degrees, worked long hours, and made money for the company.

OFFICE POLITICS

I will never forget it. Night after night I laboured over my laptop, preparing for the presentation. Then the day finally arrived. I walked into the boardroom, USB drive in hand, ready to deliver the presentation that I was sure would secure my place on the C-Suite.

I had shared the presentation with my boss several times during its development, gaining his feedback, insight, and what I thought was his support. He praised the strategy I developed in consultation with a specialist, and gave it his, "tick of approval," before the big event.

Immaculately groomed, I stood at the front of the room and confidently commenced my presentation, sure that it would be applauded by all in the room and my promotion assured.

But come slide 2, my vision of the perfect presentation had vanished. Executives around the table began to criticise my assumptions. They challenged the numbers presented and the well-researched reasons behind my approach. Worst of all, my boss, who had worked with me on the presentation and given me his approval, joined in the collective criticism.

Debate ensued, my presentation was rejected, and I walked out of the boardroom, USB in hand. I mean, who did I think I was to dare to present new thinking?

On returning to my team, they all excitedly asked me how it went. I responded, "Not that great." My 2IC commented that I seemed "fine." I explained that I was extremely disappointed. However, at that point I realised I was asked to perform a job for which I was more than qualified, experienced, and capable. I completed this task in consultation with my manager, who approved it. I was being paid to perform a task that was never going to be approved. So who is the idiot in this situation—me or them?

Almost overnight, everything turned on its head.

The colleagues and customers who supported me turned against me.

The manager I had supported year after year virtually ghosted me.

Then for some reason, the company decided it needed to complete a review of my department. This resulted in my position being made redundant, yet a new candidate was hired to do essentially my job, albeit with a new title. Interestingly, the new recruit failed to make probation and was out of the company in fewer than six months.

It was at this point I really understood corporate politics.

Corporate, or office, politics refers to individuals behaving in a manner directed by self-interest and agenda in order to get ahead in an organisation. The agenda of political players generally runs ahead of what are in the best interests of the organisation and others within it.

According to the *Harvard Business Review,* all organisations are political. This is because work generally involves people, and we are all, by nature, emotional beings who bring our own ranges of experiences, personalities, mindsets, and insecurities to an organisation.

Corporate politics, underpinned by an organisation's culture, can frustrate employees who are unwilling to "play the game" in two ways. For example, the "process politics" generally inhibits timely decision-making, is characterised by siloing information, over-administration and bureaucracy. "People politics" is the nastier version and includes favouritism, mind games, manipulation, setting people up to fail, excessive control, and backstabbing.

Most people understand that office politics is inevitable and that in order to get ahead, you need to know how to play the game. This means treading on others if that is what it takes.

From my perspective, the behaviours required to play the game were in direct conflict with my values and beliefs. So I declined to step up for selection to the team.

That experience proved a corporate career was not for me. I maintained my dignity. I knew I could not make any knee-jerk reactions because I needed the income at this point.

However, the fire inside my belly to be my own boss was flaming, and from that moment, it was not a matter of if, but when.

Corporate politics is part of the work environment; you can't escape it. It is dirty, manipulative, and evil. And from my experience, the higher you climb within an organisation, the stronger its intensity. Employees within an organisation are humans, and they each want something—money, power, status. For some, the pursuit of these goals comes at the cost of others.

For years I tried to "call out" this bad behaviour: "That's not fair." "The CEO is not a good leader." "The HR director is corrupt." But let's face it, life is not fair.

ABOUT YOU

Something made you stop and pick up this book. Perhaps something inside you is calling for change. Perhaps the title resonates with you as you walk through the airport terminal after missing your train because the babysitter was late as you took off for yet another business trip. Whether you are in corporate or working for yourself, ask yourself whether you are, "Too old for this sh*t."

Now you know a little bit about me, and it is definitely not unique or special. It is just that, my story. We all have stories. We are all born into different environments, have different culture and religions, and come from a range of lifestyles and locations.

But deep, deep down, we all want the same things: to have our basic needs met, be fulfilled, feel connected to others, and have a sense of purpose to make sure our lives mean something. Some may describe this as leaving the planet a better place because we were here.

Following are some stories of people you may also identify with.

Sandra

Sandra lives in Melbourne, Australia. She is in her early fifties, married, with two teenagers. Her husband works for a transport company and has been stood down during the COVID-19 pandemic. She was born into a fairly "ordinary" middle-class family. She attended the local public school, and then her parents made the decision to forgo some of life's little "luxuries" to send her and her brother to private high schools. Sandra enjoyed her experiences as a teen. She did well at school, hung out with her friends, did the normal things teenagers do, like skipping out to parties and drinking, but generally turned out well. As per societal expectations, she graduated from high school and was accepted into university, where she studied business. She made her parents proud when she gained a cadetship at an investment bank and established her career as a stockbroker. All sounds great right? So why is Sandra now working at a local café, waiting tables and stacking the dishwasher?

Though grateful for the income, at the beginning of every shift Sandra says to herself, "I'm too old for this sh*t."

Sam

I met Sam while seated in the back of his car. Sam is an Uber driver in Brisbane, Queensland, and a very friendly guy. In his mid-forties, Sam, his girlfriend, and their two small children live with her parents. Sam also owns a retail franchise. He invested in a franchise because he wanted to own his own business. He believed in the franchise model because of its turnkey business structure. Sure, Sam realised that there was some hard work attached, but the system was, "tried and tested," and all he needed to do was follow the steps and employ staff who would treat the business as their own. Right? What he didn't count on were staff just wanting a pay cheque and not caring about his business the same way he did, his landlord increasing the rent and insisting on a complete refurbishment of the site, and his franchisor mandating updated merchandise themes and marketing collateral each season. He is driving an Uber to maintain wage payments to his staff at the franchise.

Although Sam enjoys the conversations with his clients whilst driving his car, he mutters under his breath, "I'm too old for this sh*t."

Veronica

Veronica is in her late-thirties and met Matthew, the love of her life, when she was in high school. They married as soon as she graduated. Matthew was an officer in the armed forces, and like his father and grandfather before him, the force was his life, and he reached the highest ranks well before his colleagues. This meant Veronica, Matthew, and their three boys lived a dream life with subsidised housing and many other benefits. As a devoted wife and mother, Veronica had it all. Or so she thought. Until the day Matthew gathered the courage to tell her he had fallen in love with another woman and was leaving her. With no education beyond high school, no work experience ever, Veronica was left high and dry. While Matthew agreed to help with her rent, the lifestyle Veronica was once accustomed to had disappeared. To make ends meet, she took a job as a delivery driver for a pathology clinic.

As she delivers pathology results, Veronica says under her breath, "I'm too old for this sh*t."

Neridah

Neridah is a baby boomer in her mid-sixties and is a primary school teacher on the verge of retirement. She has loved teaching kindergarten children for decades, but even more than the children, she has loved the school holidays, long service leave, and the promise of retirement funded by regular employer contributions to her superannuation scheme. She has been planning a European adventure with her husband, Lionel, on her retirement.

As Neridah plans her final farewells to her students and colleagues, she opens the latest statement from her superannuation fund to reveal a massive drop in returns. The nest egg she and Lionel were counting on for their next stage in life is significantly less than what they need not only to fund their dream holiday but the rest of their lives. As she crumples the envelope and throws it towards the bin, Neridah mumbles to herself, "I'm too old for this sh*t."

How many of us are mumbling under our breaths, "I'm too old for this sh*t"?

PART 2
SO HOW DID WE
GET HERE?

Some habits of ineffectiveness are rooted in our social conditioning toward quick-fix, short-term thinking.

—Stephen Covey

WHEN DID I ASK FOR THIS?

When Sandra, Sam, Veronica, and Neridah were finishing school, do you imagine any of them planned these situations?

Are you able to relate to their stories and ask yourself the same question about how you came to be in the situation you are in?

Have you ever felt that no matter what you do career wise or financially, it is a case of one step forward and three steps back? Are you tired of commuting for hours each day only to deal with office politics, not being paid your worth, and ultimately not being happy because you don't have the time or money to do what you really want?

Do you ever say to yourself, "I'm too old for this sh*t," but just can't seem to find another way?

THE WELL-TRODDEN PATH

As mentioned earlier, my parents, particularly my father, had an extremely negative opinion about money, wealth, and success. In fact, referencing financial education extraordinaire Robert Kiyosaki, I had a, "poor dad." In making this statement, I mean no disrespect to my father at all. He and my mother gave me all the love and support they could. They were basing their advice on their own upbringings, advice, and environments. I am simply providing context for the opinions and values imparted on me from a very young age. I get it. My grandparents lived through the Great Depression, and this is where my parents received their "financial education." My grandparents would have been conditioned by their parents, and on it goes.

Now that I've painted a fairly bleak outlook for the careers and retirement options of Generation X, the good news is there are plenty of alternatives to the corporate workforce and being an employee.

I now have several income streams in order to spread risk. Should something untoward happen to any single income source, I have other income sources available to draw on if required. My income sources include consulting, investments, online training and network marketing.

Now before you slam the cover of this book, please hear me out. I know from years of experience the mere mention of the terms, "network marketing," or, "multilevel marketing (MLM)," has people running for the hills because they do not want to be involved in one of those "pyramid schemes."

In part 3, I take you through various aspects of network marketing. I explain what it is and what it isn't, the truth and the myths, and why I believe it is absolutely the best opportunity for the average Joe to achieve financial freedom.

I believe people do not consider network marketing as a viable alternative to the "40/40/40 scam" because of the conditioning we have experienced our whole lives. The 40/40/40 scam is a reasonably well-known phrase that refers to the most common way of working in Western societies, "Where you make someone else rich by working 40 hours a week, for 40 years, then try to retire on 40% of what was never enough in the first place—also known as a job!"

Apart from conditioning, one of the reasons so many of us believe there is no other way than to have a job is because our identities are often inextricably linked to our professions. When you meet someone you ask, "So what do you do?"

When I think back to careers classes in high school, when asked what I wanted to do to earn a living for the rest of my life, I had no idea! My father was a mechanic, and my mother was a stay-at-home housewife. Teachers said I should go to university and become a lawyer, but my self-esteem was so shot the thought of being in a huge lecture hall was completely out of the question.

I distinctly remember being handed a sheet of paper with careers listed A–Z: It started at A for "Accountant". My eyes glazed over at that point. And so my career path developed its own course. I worked hard and studied hard only to be thrown on the scrap heap!

So many of us find ourselves in similar positions. We work at a job we do not really enjoy, are extremely unhappy because we are generally paid less than our worth, and have to work within rules and limitations. Yet we seem to find it impossible to even consider another way.

SETTLING FOR COMFORT, AKA, MEDIOCRITY

People often talk of a burning platform. Of hitting rock bottom before taking action. Like people who have a near-death experience before they start taking their health seriously. People who lose everything to start over again.

Deep down, the reason a large number of us are reluctant to do anything apart from being an employee is because we are too comfortable. Comfort leads to mediocrity, which is essentially means average. Many may be content being comfortable or average, but I wanted more from life.

How many conversations among co-workers are centred around complaining about their work? It is almost a national pastime. If we are not complaining about the government, we are complaining about our employers, our employees, our co-workers, or our clients.

Really? Are our salaries really worth the emotional and often physical pain the corporate treadmill inflicts on us?

It is reported that Joseph Stalin once held a media briefing whereby he took a live chicken and began plucking its feathers in front of the crowd. This poor creature was bloodied and squawked in pain. However, Stalin continued to torture the animal until it was completely nude.

Stalin then set the poor bird down on the ground next to a small pile of grain. The chicken moved closer toward the source of food. Then Stalin took more grain from his pocket and put it out further in front of the injured chicken. The chicken clumsily and painfully staggered towards the grain directly from the same hand that moments before had caused it unbearable pain.

Although extremely brutal, this story describes how many of us are like this poor, helpless chicken. We endure the pain inflicted on us by those in higher positions for our most basic needs to be met. Environmentalist John Muir is quoted as saying, "Sheep, like people, are ungovernable when hungry,' therefore corporations 'feed' employees just enough for them to be controlled."

We, like the chicken, are enslaved to those we see as having power to control us. Each day we relinquish our power to those who rule us so long as they have the power to feed us. In other words, to provide us with an income.

The chicken is the employee, and the employer is Stalin. There is no way to rise up the ranks to be among those in power. Instead, you trade time away from your family and often negatively impacting your physical and mental well-being in exchange for a dollar amount to buy the goods and services you need to survive.

Just like the chicken, many of us hate going to our jobs. But unlike the chicken, we have choice.

Life is too short to accept being held captive to those who wield power over us. However, as employees, we are slaves to our salaries. Too afraid to raise our voices against our providers in fear of being fired. Therefore, we are willingly giving up our freedom in exchange for the illusion of economic security.

Just how secure is a job in today's environment of outsourcing, offshoring, and restructuring?

All those dreams of reaching Maslow's pinnacle of achieving self-actualisation, are exchanged to put food on the table for ourselves and our children.

We are surviving but not living. And why?

Because we have been conditioned that this is the only way to be.

Let me remind you: Go to school and study hard. Go to university and study hard. Get a good job working for someone else. Let them determine your worth. If you are able to climb ahead, it is likely you will exchange even more time and sacrifice more of yourself. Then the more you earn, generally the more taxes you pay.

And what of your identity?

How many of us identify with what we do during working hours? "I'm a lawyer," "I'm a nurse," "I'm a marketing manager," "I'm a supervisor," "I'm a …"

Whatever we title ourselves, we are still part of the millions of men and women trading not only our time for money, but the potential we hold within ourselves. Yet we call this existence a "career." An exchange of our time and often our souls for money. But we are exchanging so much more. Some of us succumb to gossip. Others work for organisations that are corrupt, yet we are too powerless to push back and risk our salary lifelines being cut off. And is that salary a true reflection of our worth and the value we provide?

And again, just like the chicken, we exchange our freedom, our health, our well-being, and our purpose for sustenance.

YOUR FINANCIAL SET POINT

The term "self-sabotage" has become fairly common in today's vernacular. But what exactly does it mean?

Let me give you an example. Have you ever thought you needed to lose a few kilograms? You get off to a great start. You've thrown out all the junk food in your kitchen and replaced it with healthier options. You prepare your portion-controlled meals ahead of time, drink lime and soda instead of alcohol when out with friends, and exercise every day. After a few of weeks, you start to notice that you are feeling lighter, the waistband around your pants is a little looser, and friends start to comment that you are glowing!

Then you are at a birthday party with some friends, laughing and catching up amidst an array of food and drink. The cake looks delicious, so you have a piece, justifying it to yourself by saying "Just one little slice won't hurt. I've been so good." Fair enough, but you know that this is not where it ends.

The next day that "one little slice" of cake turns into a glass of wine, which then becomes two. The next morning you are a little too tired to hit the gym. Before you know it, you have slipped right back into your old habits. Those pants that were feeling loose are now becoming a little snug. This is a very common example of self-sabotaging behaviour.

Self-sabotage happens when our conscious or logical minds (the part of your mind that tells you to eat healthy and exercise) is in conflict with your subconscious mind (the part of your mind that associates food with reward, and soothing stress by eating chocolate). As these two minds are at odds with each other, the critical inner voice (your subconscious mind) wins and holds you back from achieving your results by reverting to old habits.

As humans we are driven by either of two forces: to avoid pain or gain pleasure. For most people, even though the "pleasure" of having a trim, healthy body is what we think we want at a conscious level, at the unconscious level, we will do anything to avoid pain. In this example, the unconscious mind is trying to protect us from the pain of not having a piece of cake.

It commonly happens with weight loss (and gain) but also with money. We have financial set points in our subconscious minds. Say this subconscious financial set point is for you to have $5,000 in the bank. Then one day the engine in your car needs to be replaced at a cost of $3,000. And not long after, your home insurance renewal is due at a cost of $1,600. So now you only have $400 in the bank, and your subconscious is not happy! To get back to the comfort zone of $5,000, you take on an extra job and work weekends until the money is in the bank. You have been working so hard that your boss is super-impressed and offers you a promotion and a salary increase to go with it. Within a few months, your bank balance is. $8,500; life is good! So you decide to book a holiday to Fiji, which costs $3,500. And guess what? You look at your bank balance, and there it is, $5,000.

Whether you believe it or not, we all have a subconscious financial set point. For some it may be to have three months of salary set aside as savings just in case something happens. Only you determine this magic number. For many it is enough to cover the bills with just a little extra because subconsciously, this is all we believe we are worth. This also explains why money just seems to flow to the rich. It is simply because their financial set points are much higher, so their subconscious minds are having different discussions with the conscious minds, which in turn directs beliefs, attitudes, and actions. In the case of the rich, this action results in achieving wealth.

I challenge you to set your financial set point at not how much you need but how much you *want*.

From deep within, just like a helpless puppet, we are controlled by programs so entrenched and often contradictory to what we say we want that achieving success is beyond our reach. The problem is that for most of us, we are unaware of these subconscious beliefs. And as long as you remain oblivious to these beliefs, it is near impossible to reach a new level of financial success.

I know my childhood influences definitely shaped my financial set point for many years before I became aware of them, acknowledged them, and developed strategies to overcome them.

Following are some of the more common verbal programming phrases that embed themselves as subconscious financial limits in our minds:

> "Save your money for a rainy day."
> "Filthy rich."
> "Money doesn't grow on trees."
> "Rich people are greedy."
> "The rich get richer, and the poor get poorer."
> "We can't afford it."
> "Life wasn't meant to be easy."
> "This is good enough. I don't really want the bigger house, better car, or fancy holiday anyway."

Do any of these sound familiar? If you're like most people, they probably do. You're frustrated at the end of the month because it feels like every dollar you make goes towards paying bills, and you have nothing to show for your hard work.

You see things that you would like to have—seemingly frivolous items like designer shoes or a new television—and walk away, thinking that because you don't have the money now, you won't ever be able to have what you want. You're jealous of others who have achieved financial success. Perhaps you created a vision board, placing images of the house, car, and holidays you desired on a board that you looked at every day. But these things never eventuated.

While it's true that basic necessities like food and shelter cost more than ever, the real reason that most people aren't achieving wealth goals has nothing to do with how much money is in the bank. It has to do with how they think about money. Most of these beliefs are founded in fear and the need for security. Seeking security comes from insecurity, which is based in fear. More money will not dissolve the fear as money is not the root of the problem, fear is.

Fear is not just a problem; it is a habit. This habit manifested itself in behaviours that are modelled. Were your parents or other influencers spenders, savers, or risk-takers? Did money come easily, or was money always a struggle? Was money a source of joy or the cause of many arguments? Just like verbal programming, we model our behaviours around money based on what we observed and experienced growing up.

This mindset of scarcity prevents you from achieving wealth for several reasons. First, when you're constantly focused on keeping what you have, you don't seek new opportunities. So why is it that some people are destined to be rich and some are destined to struggle? Because they have different subconscious financial set points, largely based on the verbal programming they received in the early part of life. This financial set point around money is one of scarcity and is common for people in the corporate world. They are conditioned this way as promotions are scarce, resources are limited, micromanagement is plentiful, and short-term thinking is normal.

Given our subconscious minds determine our thoughts; our thoughts determine our beliefs, and our beliefs determine our actions, it is no wonder so many people never take the action required to set, let alone achieve, a higher financial set point. The subconscious mind must choose between deeply rooted emotions and logic, and emotions will always win.

The actions that manifest from our subconscious financial set points can be anything from not wanting to be financially successful for fear of losing our parents' approval, that is, "Rich people are greedy," so I don't want my parents to think of me as greedy. "Life wasn't meant to be easy," so I need to work very hard throughout my life."

People with a low or scarcity financial set point tend to play the victim—"There's no way for a little guy like me to get ahead"—because this way they do not have to take a risk, and they don't have to change. So it is much easier to stay at the level they are.

What is your current financial set point, and what results is it subconsciously moving you toward?

- Working hard for your money, or having your money work for you?
- Consistent income or inconsistent income?
- First you have it, and then you don't?
- Blaming external influences for your circumstances?

What income level have you subconsciously programmed into your mind?

- Saving or spending?
- Managing or mismanaging?
- Picking winning investments or losing ones?
- Looking at others and deep down saying to yourself, "I couldn't do that."

There are inherent differences in the subconscious financial set point of those who are comfortable having significant amounts of money and those who are not. Ask yourself whether you believe you create opportunities in your life or believe life just happens, and you just go along with it. Do you think big and play to win, or do you think small and look for obstacles instead of opportunities? Who do you associate with—people who are positive and successful or people who and negative, pessimistic, and jealous of those more successful than they are?

You may think that you have an internal driver for success. Like me, perhaps you worked hard to rise through the ranks at your corporate career and likely climbed a few rungs on the ladder. Perhaps you envisioned the view from your desk in the corner office, a team of staff running after you, and loads of important business trips.

Some of you may even have reached this. But how many of us have really earned what we are capable of earning? Or do we earn what we are conditioned to earn?

Even if we do earn higher than our financial set points, our subconsciouses will want to get back to normal, and you will be hit with a higher tax bill, land tax on an investment property, or a range of other "inconveniences" to sabotage your success and bring you back to the "comfort" zone.

Just sit back and think for a minute. Reflect on all the above and ask yourself, "Does this really make me happy?"

THE F WORD: FEAR

Like the chicken, we are afraid that if we leave our superiors, we will starve. We have been conditioned to rely on someone else for our survival.

Reliance on and attribution to something outside ourselves are referred to in strategic psychotherapy as having an "external locus of control." The concept of a locus of control refers to the degree people believe they have control over events in their lives. People with a high external locus of control believe circumstances happen *to* them, and, therefore, they are not in control. These people are more likely to conform as they tend to have a, "Why bother," attitude about changing things.

People with a high internal locus of control tend *to make* things happen. They know that they are in complete control of their lives, thoughts, values, beliefs, and actions to ensure plans become reality. These people also tend to be more confident and have a higher level of self-esteem.

Whether you have an internal or external locus of control also has an impact on your view of money and income. If you believe you are at the mercy of external sources for your income and have subconscious limits on your earning ability or net wealth amount, no action you take will change that.

Fear holds you back. So instead of becoming an entrepreneur, you develop a false sense of security from collecting a pay cheque, forgetting that you're putting your financial well-being into someone else's hands.

The scarcity mindset often makes you feel as if you aren't worthy of wealth and success. You might be focused on just getting by and avoiding imminent disaster. Never mind that there's no reason to believe that things will fall apart. You just want to stay afloat, so you're reluctant to take any chances—even if it's just investing a small amount of money. You may need that money for an unexpected bill, after all.

The scarcity mindset also causes people to make poor decisions. When you are worried about your bank balance, for example, you might put off opening the bills or pay at the last second, or even late. Yet the issue won't go away on its own. In fact, it will only get worse, thereby increasing the feelings of scarcity.

THE OTHER F WORD: FAIL

One of the reasons we avoid doing different things is because of the fear that we will fail. Fear of failure may be at the conscious or unconscious level. The reason we fear failure is that it can bring on feelings like anger, disappointment, embarrassment, regret, sadness, and shame.

The last feeling, shame, stems from worrying about what others think of you. This is generally the biggest reason people exhibit behaviours that stop them from doing things differently.

> "If I do this, my friends will laugh at me."

> "I'm not confident talking to people. I'll stammer, and people will laugh."

So you stay nice and safe in your little bubble of comfort, where you know what you are doing and who you are dealing with. You know how much money you have, and your life is dictated by this. Sure, it would be nice to try something different, but that's just not you. You couldn't risk embarrassing yourself or making people judge your abilities, so it's right for you to stay exactly where you are.

Remember that it is okay to fail. There are countless stories of hugely successful people who failed over and over again, but through strong self-belief and commitment, they achieved their goals. Just look at Walt Disney, who was fired from a newspaper job because his boss said he, "Lacked imagination and no good ideas." Steve Jobs was fired from his own company, Apple, and then rejoined it later to make it the biggest brand in the world. J. K. Rowling's novel was rejected time and time again before being published as a bestseller with the machine that is *Harry Potter* spawning movies, fan clubs, and merchandise across the globe.

Fear kills more dreams that failure ever will. And the actual reason people supposedly "fail" is because they simply quit.

If Walt Disney took the advice of his boss and quit animating, the world would not have Disney, which continues to entertain and inspire people of all generations decades after the man passed away.

The good news is that like any limiting belief, once you acknowledge it and take steps to address it, you will be surprised by the completely new perspective you have on life. More on this in Part 4.

PART 3
A VEHICLE FOR CHANGE

The richest people in the world look for and build networks, everyone else looks for work.

—Robert Kiyosaki

WHAT IS NETWORK MARKETING?

If you are like me and have been on this planet for a number of decades, there is a high probability that you have been approached by a friend or acquaintance or responded to an advertisement inviting you to take a look at a business opportunity where you can make significant income by working part-time hours around your full-time job. Perhaps you joined one of these opportunities or know a friend who did. Did you do well, or did you simply give up after a few months of seeing little reward for your investment in time, money, and energy?

Maybe some of you have never heard of network marketing.

Network marketing, also known as multilevel marketing (MLM) is actually not an industry. Rather, it is a method of direct selling used by many industries, including skincare, health and wellness, toys, business training, books, giftware, cookware, jewellery, insurance, telecommunications, and energy. Annual sales are estimated to be in the vicinity of $200 billion worldwide; it is the fastest-growing way of distributing products. There are approximately 35 million network marketers across the globe in several countries, including the United States, Australia, the United Kingdom, Taiwan, the Philippines, South America, Japan, Belgium, Spain, the Netherlands, and Taiwan.

The network marketing concept is built on providing quality products and services distributed by independent distributors, who are able to have their own businesses without the headaches of traditional business ownership. The network marketing company looks after all the back end support, such as research, production, manufacturing, packaging, compliance, inventory management, and online ordering systems.

I absolutely love the network marketing industry because of the life-changing impact it has on so many people. Life changing through fantastic products, which in my case improved my health to levels I could not have imagined. And through the opportunity to own your own business without the burden of rent, employees, inventory, and warehousing. But the best part is being able to earn income doing something I love and helping others to do the same.

FINDING YOUR WHY

A question: Why are people employees?

A. They love leaving their house every day to sit all day in a cubicle.
B. They enjoy being micromanaged, backstabbed, and treated as pawns in corporate politics.
C. They would turn up every day even if they were not being paid because they believe wholeheartedly in their employer's company vision.
D. None of the above.

Correct answer for people who are too old for this sh*t—D!

Companies purport to provide a strong employee culture by supporting their employees through employee engagement programs, inspiring them with a company vision, and expecting employees to buy into their "Why?" Don't get me wrong. I love Simon Sinek's concept of "Start with Why," but I believe we need our own why, not some company's.

In one of my corporate roles, the executive team workshopped the company's vision, mission, values, and whys. Then having congratulated themselves on this achievement, they set about "brainwashing" each staff member to believe that was the reason why they got out of bed every day to come to the office. Really?

There were umbrellas, reusable coffee mugs, mouse pads, shopping bags, key rings, and torches emblazoned with the company's "why" handed out to staff.

Staff were measured on how well they lived the "why" and the values. Try as I might, I could not replace my "why" with the company's as my reason for turning up to the office each day. Although I didn't say it, my "why" was to pay the bills, put my kids through school, and try to save for the future.

Let's face it, even when people who want to grow further in their careers, and may genuinely do so to add value and enjoy more challenging roles, at the end of the day, most people wouldn't do this unless they were paid more money. I'm sorry, but to an employee, the company is a business transaction providing mutual benefits.

WHY I'M NOT TOO OLD FOR THIS

Being your own boss is a reality for some but a dream for many. And it is definitely not for the faint-hearted. In his book, *The Cashflow Quadrant,* finance education expert Robert Kiyosaki explains the four ways to earn income.

On the left side of the quadrant are:

> E for employee—Work for someone else in exchange for a wage or salary.

> S for self-employed—You own the business but also work in the business, for example, hairdresser, accountant, lawyer, doctor, consultant. S people are often the only income source.

On the right side of the quadrant are:

> B for business owner—You own the business but generally do not work in it. Or if you do, the business is not completely dependent on you working in it all the

time. So the difference between being self-employed and a business owner is that as the latter, you can take time away from the business, and it continues without you.

I for Investor—This is where you have invested your money so it generates returns without you having to work for it.

Obviously the easiest option to earn money from the above options is as an employee. Essentially you turn up, do as you are told according to your job description, and so long as you don't steal or burn the place down, you're generally okay. Well that is if you are okay earning a basic wage, playing the game, and having the high likelihood of being replaced by a machine, offshored, or fired hanging over your head. The old paradigm of going to school, getting a university education, getting a good steady job with good benefits, working your way up the corporate ladder, and then retiring is gone, gone, gone.

I've talked about corporate politics and how people try to schmooze the power players within an organisation on behalf of their own agendas. In other words, to position themselves at the higher levels. There is generally another type of employee, one who does not play politics, nor rebuke its repugnance. These employees are effectively "hiding out" within an organisation. They generally only do the minimum of what is required, keep their heads down, and stay out of sight so as not to draw any attention to themselves as they continue to do what they are conditioned to do—go to work, take a pay cheque, and go home.

And on the topic of pay cheque or salary, employees are conditioned to expect a certain salary for the roles they fulfil within an organisation. Note this is very different from what you are actually worth; it is only what the "role" is worth. Again, the corporate structure has a tendency to benchmark people against each other. "What is the rate of pay for a marketing manager, working in a particular city with a certain number of years of experience?" There is generally a cap on this, regardless of the value you deliver or potentially could offer to the organisation if you did not have to work within the political confines of policies and rules.

As an employee, you are handing over your worth to someone else. In other words, a salary is someone else's opinion of what you are worth. Don't you deserve to respect yourself a little more than that?

Think of money as a representation of the value you provide. This definition does not equate to the definition of wages or salaries. In many cases, salaries do not adequately reflect the value someone provides; and in other cases, salaries pay much more than the value someone provides. Think of those "political animals" in organisations who rise through the ranks but deliver little. And don't get me started on the gender pay gap.

Ultimately employees are paid for their time. Whether a factory worker, who is paid by the hour measured with a time card, or a salaried employee, you are still paid for your time. You are part of the proverbial rat race and working for your pay cheque within or beyond contracted office hours. So you get up each day, commute to the office, take orders, commute home, pay bills, and rest to recharge your batteries to do it all over again the following day. That's okay. You'll get a bonus at the end of the year and a salary increase. Right?

As mentioned earlier, the annual performance review process is a relic of the industrial age. In the gig economy, it just doesn't work.

So as employees nervously prepare their dossier of achievements, documented in little boxes of "Key Performance Indicators," they must assess themselves as "missed target," "achieved target," or "exceeded target." Really? Are we still going there?

You meet with your boss, go through your self-assessment and list of achievements, and are then told that because the company didn't meet its targets, you will not receive your bonus this year, despite the fact you have gone above and beyond. Then your face turns red, your fists clench, and smoke comes out of your ears when you receive your next payslip.

"I deserve more than that," you scream to yourself. "Nobody else could have achieved what I did." This may be so, but the structure of salary reviews is often based on a matrix, where employees are literally plotted against each other to establish who gets what share of the bonus pie. Not to mention bonus payments are discretionary. Even when you do everything asked and hit your targets, payments may not be given.

I challenge you to think about a life where you create your own bonuses because

You are worth it!

You are amazing!

You deserve so much more!

MY WHY

My "why" is completely about having the freedom to live life on my terms and being true to my values. I knew towards the end of my corporate career that the politics and insincerity did not align with my values. It became increasingly difficult for me to accept income from an organisation I did not believe in. I also knew that my reason for being here was to help others—first of all my family, then those around me, and then those more broadly. And I knew I could not achieve this in my corporate career.

As I reached the dreaded middle age, I started to notice I didn't have the energy I'd like. Sure, my lifestyle was pretty hectic—a full-time corporate career that demanded a lot of my time and caused a huge amount of stress; a husband and two children with seemingly never-ending homework, sport, and other activities; a home to manage; ageing parents to care for; a social life to maintain; personal and family issues to deal with and so on. It just seemed I couldn't keep up.

And why were my favourite jeans so difficult to put on? Had they shrunk in the washing? Or was I still deceiving myself into thinking I hadn't gained weight? Of course it would have nothing to do with the daily "wine o'clock" that was just so common among my cohort of other corporate, working mums would it?

It was hard but I took a long, hard look at myself in the mirror. There were more "handles" than love. My skin had lost its glow, and I just felt like rolling over in a heap.

"What is wrong with you? You're not even fifty yet," I heard my inner voice shout.

And she was right.

I was overweight, stressed, and somewhat disengaged from life. And I wasn't even halfway there. I knew something had to change, and it had to change fast!

HOW DOES NETWORK MARKETING WORK?

Network marketing is based on the concept of building a network of many people selling a small amount of product. As your network grows, you are paid a sales commission on every one of the sales made by your distributors and/or customers on multiple levels.

It is built by providing quality products and services distributed by independent distributors who are able to have their own business without the headaches of traditional business ownership. As mentioned previously, the network marketing company looks after all the back-end support, such as research, production, manufacturing, packaging, compliance, inventory management, and online ordering systems.

The culture of network marketing is worlds apart from most corporate organisations. People are highly motivated with a, "Sky's the limit,:" attitude. You cannot get fired! Unlike most corporate environments, people involved in network marketing celebrate each other's successes, build each other up, and help each other.

Everyone can succeed regardless of educational qualifications, religious beliefs, gender, ethnicity or age. In network marketing, diversity is encouraged and celebrated.

With network marketing, your organisation builds by introducing customers and other distributors via sponsorship. If you sponsor two people to join you in business, you earn a little bit of money for everything they sell for as long as they sell. And if they each sponsor two people who sponsor two people who sponsor two people, over a period of time you have 70, 300, 1,500, maybe several thousand people in your downline or sales organisation. And you earn just a little bit of money for everything each person under you sells for as long as he or she continues selling it. That's residual income.

Perhaps the best attribute of residual income with many companies is that it keeps on paying you even after you stop working. And if you sell your business or turn it over to your children, that residual income keeps on paying, just like music royalties.

Network marketers get paid repeatedly for the same transaction. An employee who works for one hour gets paid for that hour one time. For example, an accountant spends an hour working up the company's payroll, a doctor treats a patient. Network marketers are never paid by the hour but can be paid repeatedly for one hour's work. When I started in network marketing, my first pay cheque was for $21.60. But years later, I'm still being paid on what I did that first month.

Then you also get paid not only on your results but on the results generated by others in your organisation. This mindset is difficult for employees to comprehend. It's unreasonable to think that all those people would succeed or that they would remain active; attrition is normal in any organisation. However, as long as you maintain a commitment to the simple tasks of using and recommending the product your company distributes, inviting others to do the same, and helping your team to duplicate this process, over time you will build a strong, steady organisation.

Network marketing is not just about the money. It is about the freedom of not having to have a job! It's about being able to choose how you spend your time—time with family, holidays when you want, and being able to pay your bills with money left over.

Like any brick-and-mortar business, you don't just tell your family and friends about it and then give up. No, you are in it for the long haul and won't give up within six months.

And so it should be the same with your network marketing business. Like anything worthwhile, it takes time and effort. But the rewards are so worth it!

WHY DO SO MANY PEOPLE FAIL AT NETWORK MARKETING?

Research shows that 95 per cent of people who do not buy into an idea or concept do so because they do not believe they have the internal resources to do it; their conditioning of being an employee who lives from pay cheque to pay cheque prevents this. Most people do not have the desire or the mental stamina to be their own bosses, again because most of us have been conditioned to go to school and then work for someone else. Starting and owning a business takes a significant amount of risk and self-discipline. Most traditional businesses do not make a profit for several years, if they are fortunate enough to survive at all.

The goal of network marketing is to build wealth by creating residual income based on repeat sales by a few. This is the polar opposite employee attitude of being paid for the time worked, regardless of output.

The people who fail at network marketing fail at other things, generally because they have poor self-esteem and tend to blame everyone and everything else. This indicates an external locus of control. To be successful in network marketing, you have to believe you can succeed and prove to yourself and others you believe in:

- Your product
- The opportunity

If you don't believe in it and work the business, why should anyone else?

Anyone willing to learn and put his or her ego aside can succeed in network marketing. It is a very simple business model, but it is not easy. It takes work, commitment, and above all, unquestionable self-belief. Nothing worthwhile is ever fast, free, or easy.

People are so beaten down by the corporate grind—commuting to the office, the need to get ahead, loss of self-esteem—that their attitudes take a nosedive, and so does their health.

Also, the belief that we have to identify with our jobs is annoying. Selling lipstick or weight-loss shakes as a network marketer may not sound as sophisticated as being a general manager, but with the unlimited income potential; working your own hours; no commute; and no dealing with narcissistic bosses, co-workers, and staff, I'll take network marketing any day!

Seeing others achieve great results from amazing products and helping people to overcome years of conditioning that has kept them stuck, is so much more satisfying than the results achieved during my corporate career. It is one of the most satisfying ways to work I've found, largely because I am genuinely helping others to achieve their goals. Helping others achieve time and financial freedom through network marketing really is a very enjoyable and satisfying way of life.

Over the years, network marketing has been tainted by con artists who make exaggerated claims and overstatements. This has done a lot of damage to the industry and feeds the "dream snatchers" who want to discourage others' successes. People, in general, project their own insecurities onto others.

Network marketing will work if you do! And the number one thing you need to get to work is your mind. If you like the idea and logically the business model makes sense, but you would be too embarrassed to tell your family and friends that you own your own business as a distributor for a network marketing company, then it is *you* who has limiting beliefs about the opportunity or network marketing, and so the chances of achieving success are limited from the start.

Again, anyone willing to learn and put his or her ego aside can succeed in network marketing.

We all want to feel satisfied and fulfilled in our work whilst earning money to enjoy life and ensure our security for the long term. Is doing what you're doing on the treadmill of working for an employer or trading time for money in a business achieving this?

We all trade time for money. Apart from my network marketing business and investments, I also consult. The reason I do this is to diversify my income streams so that I diversify any risk. Starting out in network marketing takes time, work, discipline, and resilience.

As mentioned earlier, there is a high chance you know of network marketing. You may have been approached or involved, or still are. There is also a possibility that what you think you know about network marketing is not accurate.

MY LIFELONG LOVE AFFAIR WITH NETWORK MARKETING

I had my beautiful baby girl in 2001. In fact, she was born amidst the worldwide chaos of September 11, and I couldn't understand why everyone was so down at the time when I was floating on air.

Becoming a mother is by far the best thing I've done in my life. It has its challenges, but the rewards and love far outweigh any sleepless nights, no matter how many years those sleepless nights last. My husband and I love our two children, who are now adults, with all our hearts. Everything we do, we do for them.

So when my best friend introduced me to a business opportunity that would allow me to work from home, not go back to my corporate job, and take care of my baby, I was all ears!

And so, my monthly order from the company I joined consisted of:

- Twenty-four cans of baked beans
- Six bottles of window cleaner

- Two packs of mascara
- 144 serviettes

Hmmm, although they are good for keeping you regular, there were only so many baked beans we could eat!

Also, as a young stay-at-home mum, I didn't know many people who would be interested in seeing my business opportunity. So after several months of purchasing products, introducing a couple of friends who were not interested, I said goodbye to my network marketing career.

When my maternity leave finished, I went back to the corporate grind, childcare, and so on. I didn't give my experience much thought for the next few years.

But that flame inside never blew out.

Years later I was presented other opportunities, opportunities with products that I really loved and that I couldn't help but share. And the opportunity came to me at a time in my life that was just perfect. In fact, people were coming to me because they could see real differences in me. I'd lost weight, I wasn't as snappy, and I was just glowing. So I thought I should have another go at this opportunity. And was I glad I did!

But although the small group of people I was associating with at my day job at the time liked my results, I couldn't get them to see the bigger picture in doing something as simple as using the products and sharing with others who might also benefit. They were just too scared of the whole network marketing "thing." To me it made perfect sense, so I decided to investigate why people didn't understand.

But then from left field, like one of those moments you see on the news and think, *Those poor people, but that would never happen to me,* it happened. An event that would change the course of my life.

As a firm believer in not being a victim, I will not divulge details of the situation. However, it propelled me on a path of discovery. A path to uncover the truth, a path to ensure that my time on this planet was worthwhile, and a journey to understand how I could help others.

This search led me in many, many directions. But my destination was psychology class to study hypnotherapy, strategic psychotherapy, and NLP.

Through this training, I was finally able to understand where all the negative connotations around money, wealth, and entrepreneurship came from. This is not about a new truth! It is about the ability to recognise and choose your perceptions and fill in the experiential gaps.

We learn from experience, not from age. But as adults, our history does not matter. History cannot be changed. As adults, at least in the Western world, we have choice.

Armed with the skills and knowledge from my psychology and hypnotherapy training, I went to work on myself and started to correct the years and years of subconscious conditioning around money, business ownership, and perhaps network marketing that had prevented my success for so long. I explored the noises in my own head surrounding wealth, as well as the common misconceptions around network marketing.

NETWORK MARKETING MYTHS AND TRUTHS

It is a pyramid scheme.

The definition of a pyramid scheme is where people are recruited solely for the purpose of making money by recruiting other people instead of making product sales to customers. Pyramid schemes are illegal and banned in most countries. Think back to the old-fashioned chain letter.

Network marketing as a legitimate business model operating in many countries across the globe. It is responsible for over $200 billion in product and service sales annually. Distributors receive commissions based on sales of products or services sold. These products and services may be sold by the distributors themselves or one of the members of their teams who are also distributors.

Only people at the top make money.

So think about the traditional business. If you are an employee in the corporate world, there is generally a structure that goes something like this.

The CEO at the top earns the most money. Think CEO of banks and other large corporations who earn salaries in the millions with bonuses on top.

The next level down is the executive team or vice presidents. This is an elite group, part of the inner circle, and privy to confidential information not shared with the rest of the company. These people are also on very large salaries and bonuses.

Another level down and you reach middle management. There are more of these than the executive/VP set. This level tends to have the greatest struggle in organisations because they are having to deal both upward and downward management levels.

Essentially the "meat in the corporate sandwich," middle management can feel like being half pregnant. You are supposed to be "strategic," one of the most misunderstood and misused terms in the corporate world, yet cannot go against any decision of the executive management, so they have little autonomy to make impactful change. You're also supposed to be "tactical" by directing and delegating your subordinates, who may not be drinking the Kool Aid and only want to do their jobs and go home.

So a lot of the time middle managers become extremely frustrated as they are in a position of appeasing those above and below, compounded by the fact that the rung on their corporate ladders appear broken as there are more middle managers, on mid-level pay, than opportunities to get to the higher echelons of the company.

The next level down is even bigger and more crowded—the staff. These people are the doers of an organisation. They have little, if any, say. And the view to the top is distant.

To represent the typical corporate structure visually would look something like this:

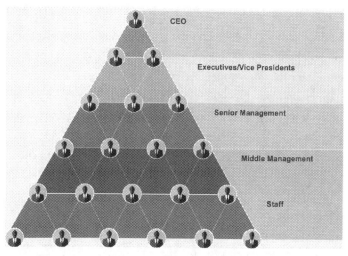

Traditional Corporate Organisational Structure

Wow. It doesn't look like a circle, it doesn't look like a square, it doesn't look like an octagon. So what does it look like?

A triangle or even worse—gasp!—a pyramid!

Now let's look at the structure within a network marketing organisation.

You have the owners and CEO at the top of the pyramid structure. Tick!

Then you have distributors recruited by the owners or founders of the company. Tick!

Next level down, distributors upon distributors upon distributors. But this is where the pyramid theory is turned upside down—literally!

Depending on how well a distributor does in his or her network marketing business, the individual's pyramid can be much larger and much more lucrative than the person who recruited that person into the business. Does this happen in the corporate world? Generally no. There may be a few exceptions—for example, a stellar-performing commissioned salesperson, such as a recruitment consultant or real estate agent, may earn more money than their manager—but in the main, this does not happen.

So now the pyramid structure in network marketing can look something like this, depending on the individual success of the distributor/business owner:

Multidimensional Organisational
Structure of Network Marketing

So here you are at the centre, and your team grows outward. Then your team members do the same. Depending on level of effort, teams can grow bigger than the person at the top and paid accordingly. I'd much rather have this pyramid than the first one!

In essence, network marketing is a matrix structure where people are connected across levels, and financial reward is via effort, not hierarchy.

Network Marketing Connects People
in a Matrix Structure

Nobody makes any money with those things.
I've tried it and didn't have any luck!

There is so much to cover in responding to this statement.

First of all, if you go into something thinking of it as just one of those "things" and putting success down to "luck," there is a high chance you will not succeed.

The reports vary, but it is often touted is that "95% of people who get into network marketing fail."

The first question that comes to mind is, "So there are 5 per cent who succeed?" I don't know about you, but I'd rather be in the 5 per cent. This is like saying, 70 per cent of adult children of alcoholics become alcoholics. Again, my response is, well 30 per cent of them do not become alcoholics.

If you look at the Pareto Principle (or 80/20) rule, this statistic isn't too far off what happens in the real world. If you look at the distribution of income, 80 per cent of people earn 20 per cent of the income (generally employees and self-employed), while 20 per cent of people earn 80 per cent of the income (largely business owners and investors).

There is no difference in people succeeding in network marketing than those who achieve greatness in any pursuit of life. What percentage of actors make it big, and what percentage spend their lives waiting tables with bit parts in between? How many athletes achieve the highest ranks within their sports because they made sacrifices and spent years training, experiencing poor results, failing, and training tirelessly to improve their games?

The biggest reasons people fail in network marketing are as follows:

- They do not set specific goals.
- They make excuses about why they are not achieving results.

- They compare themselves to others.
- They cannot deal with rejection.
- They do not treat it as a business.
- They are not willing to do what it takes—work hard for a couple of years to build wealth.
- They have the wrong mindset (that is, employee/ small business) and are unaware, unable, or unwilling to change it.
- Deep down they are happy with their lifestyles. They may complain about their low salaries, long hours, no time to spend with family, and little to no savings, but it is easier and less painful to put up with the pitfalls of being an employee than the pain of changing your mindset and doing something way outside your comfort zone for ultimate freedom.
- They quit!

I'm not good at sales, so it's just easier to work for someone else.

You do not need to be good at sales to be successful in network marketing. In fact, we are all network marketers without even realising it. Have you ever recommended a hairdresser or a great restaurant to a friend? This is all that is required in network marketing—using a product or service, loving that product or service, and recommending it to others. Then you can invite them to do the same by recommending the product or service to people they know.

Like many others, the thought of going into someone's house and selling products terrified me. At first I did what my sponsor recommended and invited my friends around to my house. I may have made one sale to the kindest friend who wanted to boost my ego, but I couldn't wait until the end of the evening to wave them all farewell from my front door.

How was I going to be successful in this business if I couldn't even host these parties?

As time went on, and after significant introspection, I realised the number one thing we all need to do is be true to ourselves. Be true to our values and play to our strengths. And one of my strengths has always been challenging the status quo. So I took some time, stepped back, and looked at the business and the world around me. Everything was online—music, clothing, groceries—so I began to build my business 100 per cent online.

First, it is far more powerful in that I can leverage my time, meeting people across locations. Second, I can work wherever and whenever I want to.

As a network marketing business owner, you choose how you operate your business, the way you introduce the products and opportunity to people, the hours you work, and the level of commitment you give. Again, like anything worthwhile, you need to be patient and give it time.

To me it just made sense. I knew that at last, I had found my freedom!

It's full of people who are fake and over-friendly.

Well if you are describing a group of people who enjoy what they do and build each other up, then yes, it is full of "over-friendly" people.

Unlike some of the toxic, political natures of many corporate workplaces, where staff either ignore each other in the hallway or push others down for their own agendas, people involved in network marketing are there to help, support, and cheer each other on. Why? Because unlike traditional corporate workplaces, in network marketing, by helping others achieve great results, everyone wins!

Like anything in life, stereotypes exist. Many people avoid network marketing posts online characterised by overuse of emojis because it feels "salesy" and "just not them". I get it. To do well at anything, you need to be authentic – be yourself. I'm definitely not "salesy". But what I am is real – and I'm really passionate about living my best life and having the time and financial freedom to live the life I want with the people I want. I lived too long playing other people's rules, knowing I would never win the game. Network marketing genuinely provides a vehicle for real people to make real money and have a great life on their own terms. This is why I work with people just like me, like you, who know they are worth so much more. My approach is no BS – just real, honest conversations and action. Not too much to ask?

The products are overpriced to be able to pay the distributors.

Think of a normal supply chain or product distribution model. The product is created from raw materials that need to be purchased from a range of suppliers. The product needs to be tested for safety and quality. It is then packaged and labelled and transported to a wholesaler. The wholesaler distributes to an online or brick-and-mortar retailer who needs to market and advertise the product. There is a cost at every stage of the process that is factored into the cost of the product.

Network marketing disrupts this model by cutting out the middlemen by shipping directly to customers and distributors and passing on a percentage of revenue to distributors as an incentive to promote the product to others. Generally network marketing companies pay distributors 40 per cent to 50 per cent of total revenues. They cannot pay much more than this without becoming unsustainable. Aside from a free coffee after purchasing ten or earning points with airlines or other retailers, what other industry gives you a share of sales just for repeat purchases and recommending its products to others?

In order to make the model work, network marketing companies require distributors to maintain a certain level of monthly product volume to be considered active within the organisation. Inactive distributors do not qualify for commission and bonuses. Generally, distributors need to spend around $150 to $250 per month of personal consumption to satisfy volume requirements to enable them to receive a bonus.

People balk at this. but think compare it to the costs of having your own traditional business, such as rent for office space or even the cost of commuting to work as an employee.

I don't want to have to host parties in my home.

Nor do I! Did I mention I was introverted as a child? I've grown to be a lot more social these days, but the idea of going to the hassle of inviting people to my house, making sure it is tidy, catering for people, and so on is not my idea of fun! Besides, it is also limiting. How many people can you have in your house? How many nights/days can you do this? And parties mean that people must be in reasonable proximity to your home. This assumes those who turn up are interested in the products or in having their own network marketing business. The whole scenario just doesn't make sense in today's world.

While I used to host home parties, I didn't find it generated any real success for my business. This is not to say other people in network marketing don't. It just wasn't the approach I was comfortable with. As I mentioned before, my network marketing business is done 100 per cent online. Because of this. I am able to reach people from multiple countries who *are* interested because they, too, are "too old for this sh*t!"

There is no competition. There are no sales quotas or targets. There are generally minimum product purchase requirements each month. However, you are consuming at least this amount each month anyway. Think of it as a much more affordable rent than when operating your own traditional business.

There are no territory restrictions. You can build your business anywhere your company has a presence. So you are not even limited by country, let alone geographic territory like a traditional sales role or even franchise business.

I don't have the time.

Of course you don't! In today's chaotic world, who does? Between a full-time job or business, children, chores, and socialising, we hardly have enough time to take five minutes to relax, let alone start, grow, and maintain a business.

I get it. I was there. But what I also eventually got was that my "busyness" wasn't actually productive, and it wasn't giving me the life I wanted. Bottom line—I wasn't happy, so I was open to new ways of thinking about life, how I got to where I was, and ways I could change things for the better. The most important change I had to make was in my mind.

Does building a network marketing business take time and effort? Of course it does. But then again, doesn't everything worthwhile take time? However, when you really think about it, all the heavy lifting has been done for you. Product development, legals, online sales, and so on have all been created. All you have to do is build a team, and with today's online world, it can be done from the comfort of your own home. You are likely scrolling Facebook, Instagram, or LinkedIn regularly anyway, so why not spend that time online more productively by building your business through these channels?

And my all-time favourite …

I don't want to have to hassle my family and friends.

For some reason, the most common reason people won't even entertain network marketing is because there is a widely held misconception that network marketers relentlessly "torment" family and friends to join their business. My answer to you is if you have this belief, don't!

I am the archetypal black sheep of my family and 100 per cent proud of it! As the only grandchild living in the city, and being at least ten or sometimes twenty years younger than my huge network of cousins living in remote towns, we just didn't really have anything in common. So for me, approaching anyone in my family is laughable. I hardly know them!

People tend to follow the lead of others, even if it is stupid. Think of peer pressure leading teenagers to engage in harmful behaviours such as drug-taking or alcohol abuse. In other words, they do not challenge or take risks to discover things for themselves. They simply watch, listen, and repeat the steps of others. In other words, blindly following without questioning is like being a sheep led to slaughter.

Many people will reject you simply because you are different. You are doing something so different to what they know or feel comfortable with—that is, it is against their conditioning. You're too happy, you're too free, you're light is shining too brightly for them! That's okay. The beautiful thing about network marketing is that you get to choose who you work with (unlike in the corporate world), and you definitely do not want to work with people who cannot share in your joy.

I have always considered myself an individual because my ideas have been way different from most of the people around me. And I like it!

Network marketing is one vehicle I have chosen to create wealth. But no vehicle will get you there if it does not have the right fuel; unshakeable self-belief is what it truly takes.

WHY NETWORK MARKETING?

Is network marketing perfect? No. However, I do believe it is a far better way to achieve financial and time freedom for the average person than a traditional job.

As a society we have been conditioned to live in a certain way. But that "way" is changing, whether we like it or not. Technology is fundamentally changing the way many of us earn a living, meaning the security of a traditional job is fast disappearing, if not already gone in many instances. If there is anything we have learned from 2020 and the impact of COVID-19, it is that nothing is certain.

Many have made the shift to a new way of work by refusing to submit to the rules that bind them. This includes moving to owning their own business through network marketing and transforming the way to earn income, create wealth, and achieve freedom.

Some of the reasons network marketing is a viable option:

1. You can start part-time around your full-time job

2. You can start building your business while you continue to learn about the products and the opportunity.

3. You can live anywhere in the world as long as you have an internet connection.

4. You can launch your business for few hundred dollars; compare this to setting up a traditional business with staff, rent, equipment, and so on.

5. You are in business for yourself, but are supported by a network of likeminded individuals wanting to help you succeed.

6. There may be tax advantages to being self-employed (check with your financial advisor as this is not financial advice)

7. By having your own network marketing business, you get the rewards from sharing the product and opportunity but not the investment and hard work that the company has contributed. You do not have to worry about product development, research, manufacturing, distribution, rent, staff, and so on.

8. You choose who you work with.

9. You receive free mentoring from people already successful in the business.

10. You are part of a positive community that is welcoming and supportive.

DON'T HAVE A PLAN B, JUST HAVE A PLAN

People often talk about having a plan B just in case plan A doesn't work out. Many people refer to their network marketing business as a plan B. What this tells me is that if plan B represents a way to achieve financial and time freedom, isn't it worth making it plan A or simply, the plan?

I also ask that if plan A (that is, full-time job that is not enjoyable, corporate politics, being paid less than you are worth, little time to enjoy life, and few prospects for anything better) is not making you happy, why is it your main priority?

I'm not suggesting anyone quit their full-time job immediately. However, I strongly recommend working on a mindset shift to focus on what is important to you and what you really want out of life. Ask yourself what you really want, not what you think you deserve or are capable of having.

Would you like to take a year off and travel the world?

Would you like to renovate your home or upgrade to a newer home?

Would you like to live in another state or even country?

Would you like to have a job or be able to earn an income that enables you to work from wherever and whenever you want?

Then ask yourself why you think you can't have these things. Is it because you believe you are not worthy; those things are only for the rich; or you just can't see a life other than your current lifestyle, that is, your plan A?

You may have seen advertisements that portray a dream lifestyle of mansions, fancy cars, and world travel, all funded by network marketing and thought, *Yeah right!* Don't get me wrong. These types of ads also raised doubts in me. However, you can generally figure out which are legitimate and which are not.

I'm not living in a French chateau or driving a Lamborghini (yet!). But it is completely possible to generate a significant income through network marketing provided you give it time, are authentic, and genuinely want to help others to achieve financial and time freedom. You also have to really believe in the products the company distributes. I have always had an interest in health and looking good, and the products distributed through the company I work with do just that!

Do you know want your plan is?

MAYBE THIS IS NOT FOR YOU

This may not be for you. Some people enjoy abseiling down cliffs, hundreds of metres above the ground, but that certainly is not for me! I completely get it that network marketing and being your own boss are not for everyone. We are all different with different needs and goals. So I want you to understand that while millions of people are successfully involved in network marketing as a lifestyle, it is not for everyone.

First, network marketing is *not* a job. Network marketing is anything but a job. No boss demands your accountability when you become a network marketer. Most days you don't have to be anyplace, such as behind your desk at a certain time for a certain number of hours. Except for the initial training with your upline, it's not likely you will have a superior telling you want to do. When you are a network marketer, you are the boss. You set your own schedule, and you decide what you will do and how you will do it.

The question is, "Can you handle that?" Because it isn't a job, you will fail if you treat it like one. Nor is it a hobby. It is a business. This means to be successful requires commitment and self-discipline. Lots of work has to be done, and you must do it without being told when and how.

If you need a structure—including an office full of people, a boss to supervise your work, and a company to provide your benefits—network marketing is probably not right for you. If you are content with a boss paying you what he or she thinks you're worth, which is rarely as much as you think you're worth, then network marketing is also not for you.

As a network marketer, you will be working by yourself with the support of your team and countless others in your company. However, if you crave the connection of having fellow employees in close proximity and enjoy "water cooler conversation" and gossip, network marketing is also likely not for you.

That's not to say network marketers are not social. Far from it! There are countless opportunities to connect with team members locally and globally through virtual and physical events. But one of the best things about being your own boss is that you choose who you associate with. Given the additional time freedom a successful network marketing business can enable, you choose who you socialise with. One day it may be friends you meet at the gym during your mid-morning yoga session or coffee with other friends not caught up in the corporate rat-race.

BE AWARE OF THE DREAM-SNATCHERS

So you've dug deep, done your research, bought and used the products, and are fairly comfortable with the compensation plan. You are super-excited and call your best friend to tell them about your new venture, who responds, "You can't be serious. Can you?"

Be aware of dream-snatchers, people who will torment you as soon as you say you're going to join a network marketing company. There are more of them than us. They are well intentioned because they do not understand. Or perhaps they may not want you to succeed.

If you don't yield to their advice, they'll turn to ridicule and start telling you that you will lose all your money because you have joined a pyramid scheme. Be polite and let them continue to collect their safe, secure pay cheque while you build your business and residual income.

Perhaps they, or someone they know, "tried" network marketing and didn't succeed. So this has tainted their views of the profession. Your critics generally can't picture themselves getting into network marketing and becoming successful, so they naturally can't see you taking that step and becoming successful. It is just so out of the way of how we have been conditioned for years that people cannot believe it.

One of the blessings and also curses of network marketing is that it doesn't take a lot of money to get started. As a result, people frequently walk away from their investment without realising what they have given up. These people never really got started. They lost interest or were discouraged by a family member or friend.

Or most likely, if they did do the work, they were discouraged by the difference between building a network marketing business and a job. They were so conditioned to receive a pay cheque for the time spent. This doesn't happen in network marketing. We are a society of instant gratification, living pay cheque to pay cheque because that conditioning is so ingrained in us we find it nearly impossible to live any other way.

If I have learnt anything from 2020, it is that relying on a pay cheque is not guaranteed. Just ask anyone in the travel industry about job security ...

YOU ARE IN CONTROL

You're in control of your own business. There are no bosses, co-workers, or employees to tell you what you can and can't do. Nobody can lay you off, transfer you, or tell you to work more or fewer hours. Your territory cannot be reassigned or downsized.

The time of day or night that you work, the marketing tools you use, the product mix that you sell, and the people you sponsor, how and when you train them are all up to you.

Most important, you are in control of you! You will likely need to learn some new skills and do some personal development work. You will need to learn how to handle rejection. You will need to learn how to stand your ground and how to keep going when rewards are not showing up in the early days. But aren't all these skills worth learning? And just think of how much you will be helping others by coaching them to do the same.

I am a firm believer of the Zig Ziglar quote that "You can have everything you want in life if you just help enough other people get what they want." I realised I wasn't really helping others in my corporate job. Sure, I was developing plans, having meetings, and sending emails, but I couldn't put my hand on my heart and say I was really impacting anyone's life in a positive way.

However, through network marketing, I am able to help people. Across the industry, network marketers help people achieve great skin, better health, cheaper telecommunications, and so on. But most of all, they help them to achieve financial and time freedom.

I want to work with others who see the vision. In other words, people who have realised they are too old for this sh*t and are willing to take action to do something about it!

PART 4
CHANGE YOUR MIND, AND CHANGE YOUR LIFE

Open your mind and watch opportunities unfold.

—Victoria Wright

YOU CAN DO IT

If you have read this far in the book, there is a fair chance some of what I've shared, if not a lot, resonates with you. You may have gone through similar experiences as the people I've talked about. Perhaps you are just wondering what the next steps are for you, and what type of world your children and grandchildren are moving into.

And you may feel that it makes sense, but there is no way you could ever replicate success outside a traditional nine to five job. I'm here to tell you that if countless others can do this, you can too!

It took me a long time to get here. Not for lack of wanting, trying, and hoping. I did everything my upline told me. I made lists of everyone I knew. I held parties in my home. I messaged people on Facebook. I started conversations when meeting with people. I did three-way calls with my upline. I sent text messages. But for some reason, I just couldn't find people interested enough to join my business. What was I doing wrong?

IT'S SIMPLE, YOU JUST HAVE TO THINK POSITIVE, RIGHT?

Over the years I have developed an interest in personal development and manifestation. I would write affirmations and speak them to myself in the mirror each morning.

"Think Positive!" "Nothing can stop you!" "Believe and achieve!" You can do anything!" I am at my ideal weight!" "I am abundant!" "Money flows to me!" And in the words of Nike, "Just do it!"

It's easy to achieve anything you want, right?

Personal development gurus and motivational speakers espouse the benefits of creating and repeating positive affirmations to achieve goals in your life, such as weight loss, career progression, and abundant wealth. Sounds pretty simple, doesn't it? And according to the gurus, they work.

Except when they don't.

Let me explain. If you already have great self-esteem, are confident, and are a consistent performer, positive affirmations may be just the boost you need to get to the gym, stick to your eating plan, or nail that promotion.

If, however, you are unsure of yourself, anxious, or even depressed, then affirmations are not only useless, they can actually cause more damage than good.

Consider a time you really wanted something to happen. Perhaps you wanted to lose a few kilograms, get that promotion at work, or purchase your dream car. If you followed the advice on affirmations, simply write on a card what you want in the present tense and repeat it to yourself over and over in your head. Some even suggested you speak it aloud in front of a mirror.

Then after weeks, months, perhaps years of doing this, you didn't have your ideal body, you are in the same job, and you are driving the same car. So it wasn't the affirmations that failed. It was you, right? Perhaps you hadn't written the affirmations correctly, perhaps you didn't repeat them often, or perhaps it just wasn't meant to be.

Stop!

The reason positive affirmations don't work is that they target the conscious level of your mind, not the subconscious. If what you are trying to affirm is incongruent with a deeply held negative belief, then all that results is an inner struggle.

Let's take body image as an example. You can affirm you have the ideal body. However, if deep down you believe you are ugly, no amount of positive self-talk will override this.

There are millions of people who believe their weight issues are a result of a family member saying to them that they were "chubby" as a child. Therefore, if you deeply believe and feel that you are destined to be chubby, even if at an unconscious level, it will set off an inner war. With each positive declaration, your unconscious will cry out, "It's not true, it's not true!" And you will find yourself reaching for that doughnut.

This conflict uses up a great deal of energy and creates massive tension in the body. The result is that the negative belief becomes stronger as it fights for survival, and what you really desire fails to manifest.

So if affirmations don't work, what does?

I am first and foremost a realist. And in being a realist, I am a proponent of brief therapy. People can overcome limiting beliefs, often at the unconscious level, first by learning they have these beliefs. Once they acknowledge these beliefs, they can then check in and validate them or not.

Because someone said you were chubby when you were eight, does that 100 per cent guarantee you will be overweight your entire life? Of course not! Your weight has less to do about someone's comments and everything to do with eating right, exercising, and getting enough sleep.

So when you have a long-standing belief, ask yourself these questions:

> What evidence supports this belief?

> Is it valid?

In many cases, it isn't. So once you understand these underlying beliefs are not valid, you can start taking action to do something about them.

This behaviour is often referred to as self-sabotage. If you do not uncover the real source of your limitations, no amount of actions, affirmations, or self-beliefs will help. As we all know, motivation is great, but it is temporary. Achieving goals takes effort and commitment. It takes regular action, even when you can't see results.

Uncovering and overcoming your limiting beliefs can be achieved in less time than you may think. You just need to find them, acknowledge them, and then do something about them.

I read books; I watched videos. I did everything the gurus told me to do. But I was still not living in the house of my dreams with the multiple six-figure income I desired. So life went on as normal. Raising my family and being part of the corporate rat-race, working forty-plus hours each week, paying taxes, paying bills; savings seemed to be harder to achieve.

My hope in writing this book and sharing my story is that I short-circuit the journey for others by explaining what's holding you back and how to change things.

IT REALLY IS ALL IN YOUR MIND

I am here to tell you the only thing stopping you from achieving your goals is your mindset. The words we say to ourselves are all that stops us from extending ourselves beyond our comfort zones.

As I said, it took me a very long time to understand this concept. It wasn't until I took my studies seriously and qualified as a hypnotherapist and practitioner of NLP that I finally got it. Hypnotherapy is a method of inducing a trance-like state that enables heightened focus and concentration. When in a state of hypnosis, you feel calm and relaxed, and more open to suggestions because it helps access the subconscious mind, bypassing the conscious or logical mind.

The subconscious mind is the part of your brain that keeps you alive. It plays a critical role in regulating functions like maintaining body temperature, keeping your heart beating, and breathing. But just as important as maintaining your physical body, your subconscious mind is responsible for regulating your mental self. Each day we are inundated with information and stimuli, and it is the subconscious mind that helps to filter that information based on the existing beliefs built up over years of experiences and conditioning. Your subconscious mind is essentially the gatekeeper of your comfort zone, which is made up of the thoughts, emotions, behaviours, and patterns that reinforce a sense of security, happiness, or wholeness in your life.

What this means is that when your conscious or logical mind is presented with a piece of information, your subconscious mind catalogues it by assigning it to one of the beliefs deeply embedded within. For example, if you see a beautiful waterfront home for sale, your immediate reaction is, "I could never afford that type of home. People like me don't live in homes like that." This is because of the deeply ingrained beliefs that have embedded themselves in your subconscious mind over many years. As described earlier in this book, verbal programming and modelling from parents around money creates a subconscious scarcity mindset. As a reminder, if you were always told by your parents they could not afford certain things and were miserly in their approach to life, you will likely have created a similar subconscious mindset.

The conscious and subconscious mind are often represented as an iceberg. Whilst our conscious mind is what we are aware of, it only makes up 10 per cent of our minds. The subconscious is 90 per cent and below the surface. It is made up of our deeply seated beliefs, emotions, habits, behaviours, values, and intuition.

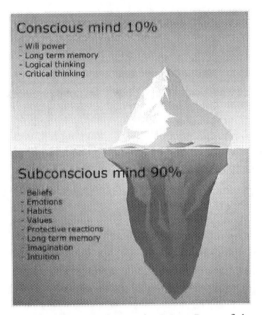

Just Like an Iceberg, the Most Powerful
Emotions Are Beneath the Surface

TAKING OUT THE GARBAGE

Being in a state of hypnosis allows suggestions to bypass the logical mind so that it is open to be "cleaned up." In other words, you are in a deeply relaxed state that can allow the beliefs, values, and memories beneath the surface to be replaced with beliefs that will serve you much better.

If you imagine trying to build a beautiful house on rocky foundations, it is only a matter of time before the cracks start to appear, and the building will crumble. This is the same with your mind. If you try to add new habits and behaviours into your life without acknowledging and addressing the underlying beliefs, values, and emotions, like the house, your endeavours will likely fail. An extremely common example of this is when people want to lose weight. Aside from any individual underlying health issues, for most people the only way to lose weight is to consume fewer calories than you exert, resulting in a caloric deficit. This makes your body utilise excess fat, and sometimes some muscle, for energy. So people will try diet after diet, take out gym memberships, and sign up for drop-a-dress size challenges. And many are successful in losing weight in the short term.

However, the "yo-yo effect" is a common phrase for a reason. A large number of people who succeed in losing a few kilograms generally put the weight back on and usually add a few extra kilograms in the process. Why is this phenomenon so common? It is because of the self-sabotage described earlier, whereby the deep-seated beliefs, values, and emotions in the subconscious mind override the conscious mind to get it back to its comfortable state. In other words, the "cheat" meals become more the norm than the exception, and workouts go on the backburner.

It is the same from a financial standpoint. Your financial set point described in Part 2 is submerged below the surface in your subconscious mind. So even when your conscious or logical mind decides to work towards financial freedom by owning your own network marketing business, unless you clear out the trash in your subconscious mind, success may be elusive. I know because I speak from experience. Whilst I loved and used the products, believed in the business opportunity, and followed all the advice from my upline, I was fighting a losing battle because of the scarcity or low financial set point in my subconscious mind.

It sounds crazy, but I realise now that every message I sent, every home party I hosted, and every three-way call I facilitated was doomed because my subconscious was telling me, *This just won't work*. I looked at the top performers in the companies I was working with and wondered, *Why can they do this but I can't?* Admittedly, there were fewer top performers than the masses of distributors, but I would later learn that this was because of the high failure rate in network marketing (as described in Part 3). But more importantly, because there are just so many of us with subconscious limiting beliefs around money and being our own boss, we find anything outside the traditional steady, secure employee mindset too uncomfortable to live with.

Although we may not realise it, many of us are running automatic negative thinking patterns that create unnecessary stress and anxiety. Common negative thinking patterns include:

> *Globalised thinking.* This is overgeneralising information and concluding that one unpleasant or negative experience will lead to a future of other failures. For example, "I'll never be able to afford a car like that." It is signified by words such as "never," "always," and "should."

> *All-or-nothing thinking.* This type of thinking describes things in black or white or extremes. You label yourself a success or a failure, yet there is nothing in between. For example, if you trip up on your diet and have a slice of cake one day, you say to yourself, "I'm a failure, so I might as well eat the whole cake," and sabotage the results already achieved.

> *Catastrophising.* This is when people exaggerate the details of an incident or situation to the most negative extreme. For

example, if you are running late for work, you may think that your boss will fire you, your wife will divorce you, and you will lose your home and your children.

Justifying. This is emotionally reassuring yourself that how you feel is an accurate representation of your reality. For example, if you feel stressed because you have a deadline looming at work, then you convince yourself it is almost impossible to overcome, and hence the stress you feel is justified.

CAUSE AND EFFECT

Leading on from the previous section, the study of successful people is essentially the basis of NLP. It analyses strategies used by successful people and applies them to reach a personal goal. As the name implies, NLP refers to the connection between neurological processes, language, and behavioural patterns that are learnt as a result of our programming and experiences. By understanding and acknowledging these patterns, we can adapt and/or replace any negative beliefs with more positive ones.

Cause and effect is a central concept of NLP. It refers to the communication pattern we have within ourselves and means that something makes something else happen. For example, "I can't lose weight, because ..." The "because" has led to the effect. The effect tends to focus on blame and the "whys". For example, "I can't lose weight because I was bullied as a child," or, "I can't be successful at network marketing because I don't know enough people."

This cause-and-effect relationship comes back to the pleasure and pain dichotomy discussed earlier in this book. We are driven by two things: to gain pleasure or avoid pain. Most people are familiar with the fight-or-flight mechanism, which represents the choices our ancestors had when faced with danger in the environment. By danger I mean being chased by a tiger! They could either fight the animal or flee. Physiologically, the body prepared itself by sending blood to the muscles required to run—or not in the case of fright.

For most of us in Western societies, the risk of being chased by a wild animal is slim to none. Instead, we have adopted the comfort zone, which means in any situation, we have the power to decide whether we seek pleasure or avoid pain. However, the question remains, Do we really have the power? Is it our conscious or subconscious mind that makes this decision?

The answer lies again in what is beneath the surface, that is, our subconscious minds which houses our beliefs, values, and emotions. The quality of our subconscious patterning determines our behaviours, decisions, and therefore, our quality of life.

It has been said that the universe abhors a vacuum. Similarly, the human mind finds it difficult to deal with ambiguity or uncertainty. To compensate for this, humans tend to fill in the gaps by making up what we don't know. In terms of subconscious beliefs relating to network marketing, here is where most of us make the leap from. In the absence of certainty, we fill the gaps of what we know, and here is where the fallacies about network marketing begin. "Well nobody makes money in those schemes." "It's a pyramid scheme, I don't want to have to hassle my friends and family." And this is where "confirmation bias" steps in. We keep running what we want—or believe—to be true.

Our biases are our projections. These perceptual errors tend to come from self-referencing from the language we hear, digest, replay, and repeat. They become beliefs that frame our conversations, feelings, emotions, and actions.

The good news is that through a series of actions based on the principles of NLP, we can rewire our subconscious mind for success.

THE CHALLENGE APPROACH

In Part 3, some of the myths of network marketing were discussed. One of the most common is that "Nobody makes any money in those things." As part of my journey of learning and discovery, I decided to really unpack this statement.

"Nobody" just couldn't be right. I have witnessed multiple six- and seven-figure earners being awarded on stage at conferences. So this was clearly a globalised statement. And as I studied more, I learnt such statements were common. For example, "All rich people are crooks."

Then through my training in NLP, I learnt to ask how instead of why. And then everything changed.

> "I couldn't possibly do that"—*except when I could!*

> "I'm not good at sales"—*except when I am because I learnt the skills and practised!*

> "I don't feel confident speaking about this business opportunity"—*except when I am*

because I listened to people successful in the
business and modelled my approach on them.

If you want to break free, always, always question your beliefs and ask yourself, "Where is the evidence?"

Traditional methods of counselling and therapy tend to focus on why someone feels a certain way. Therapists and counsellors ask clients to dig deep to find the cause of a certain belief or behaviour. This relates to the way our subconscious minds are programmed. In other words, the verbal programming and modelling of parents, which leads to a scarcity mindset and low financial set point.

However, the difference between NLP and traditional therapies is that once the why is acknowledged, NLP then focuses on the how.

Nobody—regardless of race, gender, nationality, or status—can change the past. The past is gone, the future is unknown, and the present is all we have. Therefore, there is little point dwelling on the past.

Trust me, I also learnt this the hard way!

But what I learnt through NLP was to ask myself about the how. This led me to ask how I determine everything, and I came up with what I call the "Challenge Method." Basically, I started to challenge everything!

So if you believe, "I couldn't possibly do that," challenge yourself. Have you ever done something that was a little scary because it was new? Perhaps the first day at a new job, the first time you tried a new sport?

Next time you hear a voice inside your head making a globalised statement, hearing yourself catastrophising or justifying your behaviour, stop! Stop and challenge every single part of the words you are saying to yourself and ask, "Is there an exception?" Nine times out of ten, you will be able to find it!

PUTTING IT INTO PRACTICE

A large number of limiting beliefs stem from the conditioning that "Certainty is good, and uncertainty is bad," no matter how bad the "good" is!

Applying the Challenge Method, this belief is simply not true. Uncertainty is simply uncertainty. This is because we have been conditioned over the years to imagine the outcome will be negative.

Think of this example. The company you work for is undergoing a strategic review. We've all experienced one of these, right? We receive a message from one of the assistants that our manager wants to see us in his office. Our first reaction? "This is bad news. I'm going to be made redundant. I'll never get another job. I won't be able to look after my family. I'll lose our home."

There is no such thing as certainty—except, of course, death and taxes. Other than that, to survive in this world we can only rely on one thing and one thing only—ourselves. Trust yourself more. Be comfortable with ambiguity and uncertainty.

VICTORIA WRIGHT

Ordinary people do extraordinary things every day. It is all about attitude and belief. If Columbus had turned back, no one would have blamed him. No one would have remembered him either.

The first step in changing the beliefs in your subconscious mind is to stop the excuses. Stop saying, "I'm like this because …"

I'm like this because I'm shy.

I'm like this because I have no confidence.

I'm like this because I'm worthless.

I'm like this because I grew up poor.

I'm like this because I don't have a university degree.

I'm like this because I'm fat.

I'm like this because I'm thin.

I'm like this because I'm tall.

I'm like this because I'm short.

I'm like this because I went to a public school.

Everything going on inside our heads is within our control. It is up to each of us to address the beliefs that support any biases such as the belief that "Network marketing is a scam."

Instead, create models that work for you. Most problems are based on cognitive models that are not only inaccurate but dysfunctional. In other words, they do not lead to positive well-being but focus on negative and damaging patterns of thinking, emotions, and behaviours.

Whilst our history cannot be changed, our cognitive patterns can. This is why I have chosen to focus on the how rather than the why. I focus on process rather than content, the process by which I have created and maintained my problems.

A lot of people have an external locus of control, which means they attribute things happening *to* them over which they have no control. For example, "My mother *made me believe* I was not good enough."

> "That's just the way I am; I'm just not good enough. No point trying, I always fail."
> *Except when you don't!*

I challenge you to ask yourself, "Has there been a time when you were good enough?" Think very carefully before responding. There had to be a time you were good enough for something. Perhaps you were good enough to babysit your sibling or cover someone's role while he or she was on leave.

With every statement that comes into your mind ask,

- How do you determine that?
- What evidence do you have to support that belief?
- Is it true? Can you absolutely know it's true? How do you react when you think that thought? Who would you be without that thought?

Following are some examples to help put this approach into practice:

They say? That never works? They are always?
Validate: Who says? How do you know? Are you sure?

I <u>have</u> to work in this job I hate.
Validate: Is it true? What would happen if you didn't? Is it absolutely true in all places, all times, all contexts? Does this cause you to run patterns of stress in your life?

I've failed at everything I've ever tried.
Validate: How specifically? How do you determine it's a failure? How would you know if it wasn't?

I feel uncomfortable talking to people about my business opportunity.
Validate: Which people? Everyone? Could you talk to your spouse, child, dog, best friend about it? What would happen if you were not uncomfortable talking about it? How do you determine if it is discomfort or something else? What would need to happen to make it comfortable?

Nobody respects people who are in network marketing. Validate: Who specifically? How do you know? In what context do they not respect you?

I've tried it before, and it doesn't work. Validate: What do you mean by try? How do you determine it didn't work? Did you give yourself a timeframe?

I'm not good at sales? Validate: What is your definition of "good"? How many years have you been involved in sales?

A NEW WAY OF LOOKING AT GOAL SETTING

When thinking about a new adventure or goal, I challenge you to look at it from the following four viewpoints. This will really help you to understand whether the goal is worth pursuing.

1. What will happen if you get it?
2. What won't happen if you get it?
3. What will happen if you don't get it?
4. What won't happen if you don't get it?

PART 5
MY SIMPLE FIVE-STEP PLAN TO CHANGE YOUR MINDSET

Success is the sum of small efforts, repeated day in and day out.

—Robert Collier

WHAT I LEAVE YOU WITH

As mentioned, I am trained in clinical hypnotherapy, strategic psychotherapy, and NLP. I am also a student of life and have lived through the ups and downs, ins and outs of corporate life, self-employment, financial struggle, and family drama. And I have come out the other side.

I am committed to lifelong learning and am widely read in psychology and personal development. Here are some steps that have helped me to overcome deep-seated limiting beliefs, values, and emotions in my subconscious mind, allowing me to acknowledge them, bring them to the surface, and replace them with beliefs that serve me.

1. Practice Gratitude

Just as it is very difficult to feel sad or angry while smiling, it's also very difficult to feel fear or lack while being grateful.

Practicing gratitude is one of the most widely recognised methods for improving a person's overall well-being. The practice of gratitude is based on the premise that if you look at what you have in life, you will always have more.

If you look at what you do not have in life, you will never have enough.

The way I practice gratitude is to write down at least five things I am grateful for in a journal each night. Practising gratitude doesn't mean you have to be grateful for only the big things. Most nights I write in my journal that I am grateful for my bed, clean water, food, and clothes. Of course I also include my family, my car, my clients and people who join my team. But it is completely up to you. I have placed gratitude in first place because I believe it is essential and extremely powerful in creating a positive mindset.

2. Mindfulness

In today's information overload society, it is more important than ever to take time out for yourself. Any type of relaxation, such as meditation, reading, creating art, or listening to music is a form of mindfulness.

Mindfulness allows you to take a break from the world and recharge. It is a time for you to go deep within and think of nothing but the present moment.

Looking after yourself is critical to building a successful life and business for you and your family. If you do not look after yourself, you will be no good to anyone else! Practising mindfulness can also double as a fantastic relaxation and self-care practice.

Remember, as they say on the airlines, always give yourself the oxygen first and then give to those around you. It is so important to make sure you are okay. You are no good to others if you are no good to yourself. This also applies to your physical health, so ensure you are getting adequate nutrition, exercise, and rest.

3. Mind Your Language

Listen to the words you say to yourself. Remove any negative references, whether to people, network marketing, or life in general. Perhaps ask a friend or family member point out your use of negative words.

As we know, our conditioning has been ingrained, and many negative words and phrases may almost be second nature to us. But now that you are aware of these words and phrases, just stop yourself every time they pop into your head. Stop and challenge them. If the words and thoughts you speak to yourself are valid and serve you in a positive way, keep listening to them. If, on the other hand, they are negative and not serving you, stop, listen, challenge, and correct them.

4. Make a Plan to Achieve Your Goals

Making concrete plans is one of the most practical and empowering things you can do to effect a mindset shift. It involves moving away from the victim position. Instead, view yourself as someone who is capable of taking action to change things. After all, creating plans involves becoming active rather than reactive.

If you have a large goal and feel intimidated by the idea of making a plan, try splitting it up into a series of smaller goals, and then make a plan for each of these subgoals. Each time you tick off a subgoal, allow yourself to feel proud of the progress you're making towards your bigger aim.

I also take a deeper view of goal setting by really analysing whether the goal is something I really want. By doing this, you can uncover any limiting beliefs up front that may appear as self-sabotaging behaviours throughout the journey to achieving your goals.

5. Get Uncomfortable

Do something each day you wouldn't ordinarily do. For example, strike up a conversation with a stranger in a coffee shop, or challenge your neighbour to a game of tennis. It can even be as simple as using the other hand to brush your teeth! By taking small steps to move beyond your comfort zone, the ingrained beliefs you once held will gradually shift because you will prove to yourself that anything is possible if you have the right mindset and commitment.

I hope my story has resonated with you on some level. Whether network marketing is the right vehicle for you is something only you can decide. For me it just makes sense and is a viable method to create wealth without the grind of being an employee or the risk of being a traditional business owner.

JOIN MY TEAM

If you would like to find out more about the network marketing company I work with and/or would like to join my team, please visit my website, www.victoriawright.com.au to make contact.

My team is built with people who have opened their minds to the reality of making money outside the "traditional" nine-to-five. It is not an "all or nothing" situation – many people simply share the product with a few others, and gradually build a team with loyal users and advocates of network marketing.

I'm not suggesting it will be easy – but then nothing worthwhile ever is. For example, dealing with rejection from people who may disagree with you is not only character building, it helps you to improve your skill and before you know it, you will be building your team as if on autopilot! Using this book to share the message is a great tool to help others who may not quite understand the concept because they have listened to 'naysayers' for too long.

It is important to really believe in the products of the company you are associated with – most network marketing companies have extremely high quality products. This is because advertising spend is diverted via word-of-mouth, allowing companies to invest in research and development. I work with a health and wellness company so there are plenty of products for everyone to look and feel their best. The most important thing we have is our health. Without our health, nothing else matters.

And remember, it isn't just those who are "too old for this sh*t" either. There is a growing movement of young people who do not want the life of "struggle" and frustration of their parents, but instead are building serious businesses in network marketing, with the income to match.

So, are you ready to challenge your beliefs and step outside your comfort zone – just in case you may actually like what you see?

Please feel free to reach out to me by visiting:

www.victoriawright.com.au